ISLAND HARVEST

ISLAND HARVEST

OVER 100 FRESH NEW RECIPES

Nick Nairn

Photographs by Jean Cazals

Published by BBC Worldwide Limited,
Woodlands, 80 Wood Lane, London W12 0TT
First published 1998
Reprinted 1998
First published in paperback 2000
© Nick Nairn 1998
The moral right of the author has been asserted.

Photographs by Jean Cazals, © BBC Books 1998

ISBN 0 563 38422 0 (hardback)
ISBN 0 563 55155 0 (paperback)

The quote on page 6 is reproduced by the kind permission
of Faber & Faber Limited

Commissioning Editor: Nicky Copeland
Project Editor: Khadija Manjlai
Copyeditor: Christine King
Art Director: Frank Phillips
Designer: Isobel Gillan
Stylist for photography: Antonia Gaunt
Home Economist for photography: Debbie Major

Set in Futura and Fairfield
Printed and bound in France by Imprimerie Pollina s.a.
Colour separations by Radstock Reproductions Limited,
Midsomer Norton

Dedicated to Bunty

ACKNOWLEDGEMENTS

I'd like to thank all the folks at Ideal World, especially
Hamish Barbour, Peter Jamieson and Carl Hindmarch for
making *Island Harvest* such a cracking series. Special
thanks to Debbie Major for all her help with testing the
recipes and for being able to read my writing; Fiona
Buchanan, my long-suffering assistant, for allowing me to
meet my deadlines; Andrew Meehan for his continuing
creative inspiration; and the team at BBC Books, notably
Nicky Copeland, Frank Phillips and Khadija Manjlai.

A Personal Note from Nick Nairn About Beef on the Bone
*'Although there has been major concern over sales of beef
on the bone, my opinion of the government's blanket ban is
that it is a knee-jerk reaction. No differentiation has been
made between native cattle, farmed organically by small
producers, and intensively reared continental breeds,
which are not fed naturally and have to be overwintered
and fed on pellets and grain. Should the ban be reversed,
I would urge everybody, everywhere, to buy the beef of
such native cattle as Aberdeen Angus, Galloway or
Shorthorn – sturdy wee coos fed on grass. Ultimately,
though, the decision rests with you, the consumer.'*

Previous page: *Seared Scallop Filo Tartlets with Basil,
Tomato and Caramelized Onion* (page 32)

CONTENTS

INTRODUCTION

How's your carrot?
It's a carrot.
So much the better, so much the better.

Waiting for Godot, Samuel Beckett

It shows how far we've all come when a self-taught chef like me can harp on in public and in print, and not be hounded out of the place in a hail of couscous, Puy lentils and half-eaten banana tarte tatins. But, it seems, we're no longer preaching to the unconvertible.

There's a real sense of change pulsing through Scottish food culture. Chefs all over the country are getting hold of the best raw produce they can find and working wonders with it – which shouldn't be too hard, as what makes Scottish cooking unique is what makes it universal: fine produce. After all, you don't have to be a person of consequence to make the best out of good ingredients.

I'm under no illusions, however. Some people continue to torture some of the finest food on the planet into the most illogical shapes and daffy combinations. Of course, some things will never change. During the filming of the TV series on which this book is based I tasted some pretty dodgy food served in restaurants and hotels which, having access to such good produce, should know better. But let's leave them to it. Welcome to *Island Harvest*.

I can't think of anything finer than messing about in boats off the west coast of Scotland. You've just had a steaming plate of *Razor Clam Risotto*, the sea is so blue you want to wear it, and the sky is bathed in that lambent, smoky light you don't get anywhere else. Dreadful things could be happening in the world and you just can't work it up to care. You're in heaven.

So, what's changed this time around? Well, cooking on a boat can be a tricky situation at the best of times. Add the nervous energy of a television crew and you're guaranteed to be pumping adrenalin. We held our own though, and the ideas within these pages are, I think, the most straightforward and my best yet. Alongside the likes of *Roast Loin of Hare on Truffled Spinach with Horseradish Mash* is *Harissa Chicken with Couscous and Lemon and Cumin Yoghurt*. They draw on different traditions but I'm not yoking together disparate cultures for the sake of it; this is fusion food.

But you can also take the low road and head for the homemade oatcakes or *Mull Cheddar Omelette*. There's no secret formula or magic potion. Good food shouldn't be treated like a Fabergé egg. *Island Harvest* is a compendium of all the things I enjoy about cooking – informality, spontaneity and generosity. I've also tried to combine the attributes of ingenuity and simplicity, classicism and open-mindedness. I hope you enjoy the results.

Salmon Sushi (page 33)

USEFUL EQUIPMENT

Getting yourself quality gear means saving time and effort on the day, so it's worth treating yourself – even if you have to do so in instalments.

Blowtorch This is a perfect tool for finishing off crème brûlées and roasting red peppers and tomatoes, but you can of course get by with a grill.

Cast-iron griddles A ridged griddle is great for roasting vegetables and getting that criss-cross char-grilled effect on meat and fish. Smooth griddles are excellent for making scones. It's best to get good, heavy-based ones, preferably with metal handles so that they can go in the oven as well.

Chopping boards Ten years ago the environmental health people said that we should use plastic chopping boards rather than wooden ones. Plastic boards are terrible! They blunt your knives and they retain the smell of food, so they taint what you're chopping. Now the health police have relented, thank goodness, but here are a couple of hints regarding wooden boards: wipe them down but don't put them in the dishwasher as they warp. A wet tea towel under the board when you're using it keeps it firmly in place and nice and level.

Crockery It's much easier to make food look attractive on big white plates. Don't spend a fortune on crockery and have the food looking cluttered on the plate because of the pattern. Let the food speak for itself.

Electric whisk A hand-held one gives you more control than a mixer when you're making things like meringue. It's also easier to clean than a mixer and it saves you bulging, aching biceps.

Electronic scales For precision measuring. Commercial kitchens wrap them loosely in clingfilm and use them as normal. This stops all the debris of the kitchen getting into the gubbins of the scales.

Food processor Indispensable for soups, pasta, breads, pesto, breadcrumbs...the list goes on and on. It really takes a lot of the hard graft out of cooking. The only drawback is that food processors are a bit fiddly to clean, so I use one only for medium or large batches of food.

Frying pans The best ones to use are black iron. After being seasoned they are superb for cooking with – and they last for ever. As well as these you can get really good-quality stainless steel non-stick pans. Never buy a cheap non-stick pan because the non-stick surface will come off in bits in an outrageously short time, so buy the best you can afford. Polaris is a very good brand to look out for, Marks & Spencer have a very good one or, if you're feeling minted, Wohl pans have a titanium-bonded surface which never comes off.

Garlic press A good-quality non-stick one. I used to hate them, but actually they're quite useful.

Hand-held blenders Also known as 'stick-liquidizers', these small electric liquidizers have revolutionized sauce-making, allowing anyone to make light, frothy sauces and banishing split sauces to a thing of the past.

Kilner jars These swing-top jars with replaceable rubber seals are handy for storing pesto, home-dried tomatoes and practically anything else you can cram them with. Just make sure you give them a good wash and dry them well before use.

Knives Spend the most money that you can afford on knives. A large 25–30 cm (10–12 inch) knife, a flexible boning knife and a steel for sharpening will aid your cooking no end. Learning how to use the steel takes practice but it's essential for maintenance of your blades. Hold the steel upright with your hand behind the guard and put the base of the knife at the base of the steel at an angle of 20 degrees. Using long strokes, pull the knife up the steel so you go from base-to-base in contact, to tip-to-tip in contact. Then turn over and do the same on the other side. The steel sets up an electromagnetic force that realigns all the molecules at the edge of the blade – and it just takes any wee dings out. You're stopping the knife from going blunt, you're not sharpening it. Once a knife is blunt, a steel won't sharpen it.

Le Creuset terrine This is a wonderful piece of kitchen equipment. I prefer Le Creuset terrines over any other because they are cast iron, which means they don't warp, they conduct heat evenly around the whole terrine and they will last you through to the next ice age! All the ingredient quantities for terrines in this book are based on a Le Creuset terrine capacity.

Mandolin graters Plastic versions are a good introduction to using mandolins but, if you can afford it, try and get a Braun mandolin – it's the one that professional chefs use and it does cost mega-bucks (about £100!), but it's possibly one of the most useful tools in the kitchen. Watch your fingers though, and fling away that last bit of food unless you want to incorporate your fingertips in the dish that you're making.

Omelette pan A 20 cm (8 inch) pan makes a perfectly sized omelette for one and it's also useful for dry-roasting small amounts of spices. Get one with a non-stick surface and a heavy base if you can.

Pasta machine Indispensable for fresh pasta. If you don't use your machine regularly, make sure you oil the rollers, otherwise they will seize up. Use a wee bit of vegetable oil for this, not WD 40! On the same note, the first time you use the machine, put through a disposable batch of dough as there's always oil on the rollers which will taint your first lot of pasta.

Pepper grinder To get a really good pepper grinder, make sure that it has a Peugeot mechanism in it…they're the best by miles.

Plastic spatula or spoonula Great for scraping every little bit from mixing bowls. It will pay for itself in months.

Rolling pin I prefer the polythene ones because they don't stick so much and don't dent so easily.

Scone or pastry cutters Much beloved of the presentation brigade, myself included. They are great for creating the beautiful towers of food that we love so much.

Seasoned baking trays Like pots and pans you should consider this as an investment – the more you bake with it the more like an old friend it will become. Treat it well and it will last for ever (or nearly). Silpat is a flexible silicon mat, a nifty little piece of equipment that chefs use for brandy snaps and biscuits, etc. and you can get something similar from cookshops and some supermarkets now. Nothing sticks to the mat, but it won't stop things burning if you're not looking out for them.

Sieves The chinois is a fine, metal, conical sieve. Very handy for straining stocks, sauces and sorting out any lumpy sauce (yes, even for me, folks!). To get the best from your chinois, wash it as soon as you've used it, otherwise all the holes clog up and it becomes knackered. A conical strainer with larger holes is great for sieving mashed potatoes and straining soups and, although quite expensive, lasts for ever.

Sushi mat A handy wee tool for making sushi. You can get them from most Chinese supermarkets and they cost only a quid or so. They are made from thin strips of bamboo woven together into a flexible mat, designed specifically for rolling perfect cylinders of sushi and that's what sushi is all about: perfection.

Wok A wok is the best and safest thing to use for deep frying. Its sloping sides mean that the oil can expand outwards when it gets hot. Steep-sided pans give the oil nowhere to go except up – very tricky!

Zyliss cheese grater (râpé) Brilliant for chocolate or fresh Parmesan. You can keep the cheese in the grip at the top and store the whole thing in the fridge.

Other useful pieces of equipment include: a good-quality lemon zester, a canelle cutter, measuring jugs, a set of ramekins, metal or glass mixing bowls, a waiter's friend (one of those nifty all-in-one corkscrews that is shaped like a pen knife) and a little coffee grinder for grinding spices.

STORECUPBOARD INGREDIENTS

Having the right things in your storecupboard makes it much easier to throw together an excellent meal with hardly any notice. You've got to admit it's far nicer to come home and have something delicious, rather than a piece of frozen chicken and a can of baked beans.

In your fridge

Bulb of garlic Fresh is preferable, and is usually available in early season, around April.

Butter (unsalted), which also freezes well. Many butter producers have come up with a piece of inspired packaging – they've marked 25 g (1 oz) notches on the wrapper so that you know how much to cut without worrying about scales…a touch of genius.

Chillies Supermarkets generally have a heat scale on packets of chillies as a guideline, but the trick is to taste what you're making all the way through, so you can't go wrong.

Eggs If you can get your hands on eggs straight from a farm where the chooks run round free, you are in luck. The difference in quality between these eggs and even supermarket free-range eggs is huge: the yolks are a fantastic orange colour, and the flavour is something else. Once you've tried them, you'll never look back.

Fresh herbs, which keep for up to four or five days in the little trays that you get them in. If you can, though, have some growing. They make such a difference to the flavour of a dish. Rosemary, thyme and mint all grow like wildfire if you give them a chance.

Fresh root ginger

Home-dried tomatoes (see page 184)

Lemons and limes

Pesto

Reggiano parmesan cheese Get a nice block of it.

Tapenade

White wine A couple of bottles are always handy.

In your freezer

Butter Unsalted.

Olive oil Freeze some in an ice-cube tray. Little cubes of unctuous flavour.

Pesto Freezes well in the same way, and the cubes don't lose their colour.

Pine kernels Strangely, this is the best place to keep them fresh.

Stock Home-made or bought. Supermarkets are increasingly producing good-quality, fresh stocks that keep very well in the freezer.

In your cupboard

Balsamic vinegar Buy the best you can afford.

Black and white peppercorns The important thing to remember about pepper is that it must, must, must be freshly ground. The pre-ground stuff is too fine and it goes stale very quickly.

Chilli and black bean sauce This stuff packs a punch! You can get it from Chinese supermarkets. Try and get the proper Chinese version as it has a much better flavour.

Chocolate Look for one with a minimum of 60 per cent cocoa solids.

Curry pastes Good-quality ones.

Dark soy sauce I find Kikkoman's is good.

Dried egg or rice noodles Those 4-minute ones are great.

Dried pasta

Flour Self-raising, plain and wholemeal.

Gelatine Sachets of powdered gelatine, or leaf gelatine if you can find it.

Honey Use the clear, runny type.

Maldon salt In most of my recipes you'll see that Maldon salt is almost ubiquitous. I prefer it above processed salt and coarse sea salt because the soft flakes of Maldon give lovely frissons of flavour in your mouth – they really have that iodide flavour of the sea.

Olive oil Really you want to have two kinds of olive oil: one cheaper kind for general use, and a really top-notch one, preferably an estate oil from a single producer. The good-quality oil, with its deep colour and rich, peppery flavour, is perfect for dressing salads and drizzling round dishes like risotto.

Red wine vinegar Preferably Cabernet Sauvignon vinegar.

Rice Arborio and basmati.

Spices Paprika, chilli, saffron, whole nutmegs, cinnamon, cloves, star anise, cumin and coriander seeds, turmeric, etc. I buy whole seeds and grind them myself in a coffee grinder when I need them. This serves two purposes: it stops them going stale so quickly and it also allows you to get full flavour out of them by dry-frying them whole before you use them.

Stock cubes Chicken stock cubes are good all-rounders for emergencies – try and use the best quality you can find. They're really good for dishes such as risotto which is finished with lots of highly flavoured ingredients that would mask the taste of fresh stock.

Sugar Natural brown sugar, such as muscovado, has much more flavour than white. Also keep icing, granulated and caster sugar.

Sunflower oil

Tabasco

Thai fish sauce This is made from fermented fish and, used in small quantities, it adds a piquant flavour to a dish.

Tins of chopped tomatoes

Tins of precooked pulses Tins of chickpeas, kidney beans or butterbeans just take the hassle out of 24 hours of soaking. Give them a good rinse under the tap before you use them, though, as the liquor they're kept in is full of sugar and salt.

Tomato ketchup Add it to tomato sauces for sweetness – it balances the acidity of the tomatoes.

Wine It's always nice to have a few bottles of wine knocking around in the kitchen as they can add a wonderful dimension to some dishes – and of course you'll have something to sip while you're cooking. Never cook with wine you wouldn't drink yourself, so you just need to find another use for that Matteus Rosé your Aunty Hilda gave you for Christmas last year. I usually have a couple of bottles of red Burgundy and Californian Chardonnay in my store-cupboard, but for some reason they never seem to last long.

Worcestershire sauce

NOTES ON RECIPES

Before you start using this book, please note the following:

- Eggs are large unless otherwise stated. Buy farm-fresh eggs laid by chickens allowed to run around free. The difference in quality between these eggs and even supermarket free-range eggs is huge: the yolks are a brilliant orange colour and the flavour is exceptional.

- At the time of going to press, the government had just introduced a ban on the sale of beef on the bone. This book, therefore, contains recipes using beef on the bone. See also author's note on page 4.

- Spoon measurements are level. A tablespoon is 15 ml; a teaspoon is 5 ml.

- Conversions are approximate and have been rounded up or down. In a few recipes it has been necessary to modify them very slightly. Follow one set of measurements only; do not mix metric and imperial.

- Oven temperatures and cooking times are flexible and may vary according to the equipment and ingredients used.

- Wash all produce before preparation.

Scotland's lush land – sometimes

bathed in sunlight, at times washed

by soft rain – produces some of the

world's best crops; even the weeds

hold great promise.

SOUPS

NETTLE SOUP

with warm soda scones

This was a real revelation when I tasted it made by Heather Dewar in her tiny cottage overlooking the Sound of Jura. The secret is to use just the tips of young nettles – strong gloves and sharp scissors are a must here. The finished soup has got a lovely mineral flavour – and no, it doesn't sting your lips!

Serves 4

50 g (2 oz) butter

1 large onion, chopped

450 g (1 lb) potatoes, peeled and diced

1 large leek, cleaned and sliced

600 ml (1 pint) Chicken Stock (see page 181)

450 g (1 lb) young nettles

Maldon salt and freshly ground white pepper

4 tablespoons crème fraîche

For the soda scones:

225 g (8 oz) plain flour

1 teaspoon bicarbonate of soda

1 teaspoon cream of tartar

½ teaspoon Maldon salt

scant 300 ml (10 fl oz) buttermilk, or fresh milk
   soured with a little lemon juice

Bring a large pan of water to the boil. Melt the butter over a low heat in a second pan, add the onion, potatoes and leek and cook gently for 10 minutes until softened. Add the stock, bring to the boil, cover and leave to simmer for 15–20 minutes until the vegetables are just cooked. Meanwhile, put on a pair of rubber gloves and pick the nettle leaves from their stalks. Wash them well, drop them into the pan of boiling water and cook them for just 60 seconds. Drain them immediately and refresh under cold water. Squash them into a food processor and blend them into a smooth purée. Tip this into a jug and set aside.

For the scones, heat a smooth griddle over a medium–high heat. Sift the flour, bicarbonate of soda, cream of tartar and salt into a bowl. Gradually stir in enough buttermilk or milk to make a moist, but not wet, soft dough. Turn out the mixture onto a surface lightly dusted with flour and shape into a round about 2.5 cm (1 inch) thick. Cut this into 4 or 6 wedges, lift them onto the griddle and cook them gently for 10–15 minutes on the first side until golden brown. Turn them over and cook them for another 5 minutes. Keep them warm.

Liquidize the soup until smooth. Return it to the rinsed pan, stir in the nettle purée and season to taste with salt and pepper. Reheat the soup gently but do not allow it to boil or you will lose its beautiful, vivid green colour. Serve in warmed soup bowls with a spoonful of crème fraîche in each and the warm soda scones.

BUTTER BEAN SOUP

with chilli and deep-fried chorizo

This majors on big robust flavours and uses my favourite pulse, the underrated butter bean, which makes a gorgeously creamy base for this soup. The parsley, lemon and garlic mix which you bung in at the end is in fact the classic Italian flavouring called gremolata. Normally it's added to osso bucco, but here it brings all the other flavours alive with its tangy freshness. Use thin slices of big chorizo for the garnish so they end up a bit like big meaty potato crisps once fried. (Got that idea from eating a pepperoni pizza on the way back from the pub one night. I picked off all the crispy sausage and binned the stodgy base – amazing where we chefs get our inspiration.)

Serves 6-8

225 g (8 oz) dried butter beans

150 ml (5 fl oz) olive oil

2 onions, peeled and chopped

4 cloves garlic, crushed

2 teaspoons harissa or minced red chilli
   from a jar

1 teaspoon paprika powder

½ teaspoon ground cumin

a good pinch of saffron stamens

1.5 litres (2½ pints) Chicken Stock
   (see page 181)

2 fresh bay leaves

finely grated zest of ½ small lemon

3 tablespoons chopped fresh flatleaf parsley

2 tablespoons lemon juice

Maldon salt and freshly ground black pepper

sunflower oil for deep frying

18–24 very thin slices chorizo sausage

a little extra virgin olive oil, to serve

Cover the butter beans with plenty of cold water and leave to soak overnight. The next day, heat the olive oil in a large pan. Add the onions and fry for about 10 minutes until soft and golden. Add half the crushed garlic and the harissa or chilli and fry for another 2 minutes.

Add the paprika and the ground cumin and fry for 1 minute, stirring. Drain the beans and add to the pan with the saffron, chicken stock and bay leaves. Bring to the boil, cover and leave to simmer for 45 minutes or until the beans are very soft.

Mix the remaining garlic with the lemon zest and the chopped parsley. Stir this mixture into the soup and liquidize in batches until smooth. Return to the pan, add the lemon juice and some salt and pepper to taste and keep hot over a low heat.

For the garnish, pour about 2.5 cm (1 inch) of sunflower oil into a pan and heat to 180°C/350°F. Separate the chorizo slices and fry a few at a time for about 15 seconds until crisp and lightly golden. Lift out with a slotted spoon and drain on kitchen paper.

Spoon the soup into warmed soup plates and pile some of the deep-fried chorizo slices into the centre of each bowl. Drizzle the soup with a little extra virgin olive oil and serve.

CHILLED CUCUMBER AND YOGHURT SOUP

with seared langoustines

This is a beautiful soup for a warm summer's day – tasty, refreshing and pretty to look at too. It also uses my favourite combination of hot and cold in the same dish. You could serve it with or without the langoustines, or substitute raw tiger prawns instead. Make sure that the stock isn't too strong or it will overpower the other more delicate flavours – the tubs of ready-made supermarket chicken stock are perfect for this recipe.

Serves 4

2½ cucumbers
300 ml (10 fl oz) Greek natural yoghurt
300 ml (10 fl oz) Chicken Stock
  (see page 181)
75 ml (3 fl oz) crème fraîche

a few drops of Tabasco sauce
Maldon salt
2 tablespoons chopped fresh mint, chervil,
  chives or dill, or a mixture if you prefer
6 langoustine tails
2 tablespoons olive oil

Peel 2 of the cucumbers, cut them in half lengthways and scoop out the seeds with a melon baller or teaspoon. Roughly chop the flesh into small pieces and liquidize in batches in a liquidizer or food processor with the yoghurt, chicken stock, crème fraîche, Tabasco sauce, 1 teaspoon salt and herbs until really smooth. Pour the soup into a bowl, cover with some clingfilm and chill in the fridge until very cold.

Bring a large pan of lightly salted water to the boil. Add the langoustine tails, bring them back to the boil and then drain. Refresh in cold water. When they are cool enough to handle, peel off the shells and cut them in half lengthways. Peel the remaining cucumber, cut it in half and scoop out the seeds. Cut the flesh in long, thin ribbons and dry them on some kitchen paper.

Just before you are ready to serve, heat the olive oil in a large frying pan, add the langoustine halves and stir-fry over a high heat for 1 minute until just cooked. Season with a little salt.

Ladle the soup into large, chilled soup plates and pile some of the cucumber ribbons into the centre of each bowl. Arrange 3 of the hot langoustine halves on top of each portion and serve.

EMERALD GREEN POTATO AND WATERCRESS SOUP

The great things about this soup are its bright green colour and earthy, slightly metallic flavour which you achieve by adding the watercress at the end of cooking, thereby keeping both its colour and its flavour. The idea was stolen from my friend Paul Rankin, an Irish wonder-chef and a man who really understands food. He's still a big Irish galoot though! While on the subject of plagiarism, the idea of adding the spinach at the end of cooking belongs to another pal, Phil Vickery, a lad who can cook a bit and is an arch rival on *Ready Steady Cook*. I wish he'd stop beating me!

Serves 6

175 g (6 oz) butter
750 g (1½ lb) floury main crop potatoes, such as Maris Piper or King Edward, peeled and thinly sliced
1.75 litres (3 pints) boiling water

350 g (12 oz) watercress, stalks and all, roughly chopped
50 g (2 oz) spinach, washed and any large stalks removed
Maldon salt and freshly ground white pepper
6 tablespoons double cream and watercress sprigs, to garnish

Melt the butter in a large pan. Add the potatoes and stir well so that they all get well coated in the butter. Cook over a very gentle heat for about 6 minutes until they are slightly softened and starting to break up. Then increase the heat, add the water and bring to the boil. Cover and leave to simmer for 20–30 minutes until the potatoes are very soft.

Stir in the watercress and cook for just 3 minutes. Stir in the spinach and, as soon as it has wilted into the soup, liquidize it (in batches if necessary) until smooth. Return to the pan, season with salt and plenty of ground white pepper and bring back up to temperature.

Pour the soup into heated serving bowls and garnish each portion with the cream and a couple of sprigs of watercress.

SPICY AUBERGINE AND TOMATO SOUP

with minted yoghurt

Aubergines love spices and tomatoes, so this soup's off to a great start. The minted yoghurt garnish tempers things a bit and provides that much-loved (by me) temperature contrast. Use a good-quality curry paste as hot or as mild as your taste prefers. Personally I've come to love the combination of coriander and basil – a real East meets West thing – but you could use just one or the other with equal success.

Serves 6-8

2 large aubergines, weighing about
   225–275 g (8–10 oz) each
300 ml (10 fl oz) olive oil
2 red onions, peeled and sliced
1 tablespoon cumin seeds
2 teaspoons coriander seeds
1 tablespoon hot curry paste
2 teaspoons fennel seeds, finely ground
3 cloves garlic, crushed

400 g (14 oz) can chopped tomatoes
1.2 litres (2 pints) boiling water
Maldon salt and freshly ground black pepper
2 tablespoons chopped fresh coriander
2 tablespoons shredded fresh basil

For the minted yoghurt:
6 tablespoons natural low-fat yoghurt
1 clove garlic, crushed
1 tablespoon chopped fresh mint

Cut the aubergines into 2 cm (¾ inch) thick slices. Heat 50 ml (2 fl oz) of the olive oil in a large pan, add a layer of aubergine slices and fry for a few minutes until lightly browned. Then turn them over, add a splash more oil and fry once more until golden. Lift out onto a plate and repeat with the rest of the aubergines and some more of the oil until they are all cooked.

Now add the remaining oil and the red onions to the pan and fry for 5 minutes until soft and lightly browned. Meanwhile, heat a dry frying pan until quite hot. Add the cumin and coriander seeds and toss them around for a few seconds until they darken slightly and start to smell aromatic. Tip them into a coffee grinder or pestle and mortar and grind them to a fine powder. Add the curry paste, roasted cumin and coriander and the ground fennel to the onions and fry for 2 minutes, stirring now and then. Add the garlic and cook for 1 minute.

Roughly chop the aubergines and return them to the pan with the chopped tomatoes and the water. Bring to the boil, cover and leave to simmer for 20 minutes.

Now you need to liquidize the soup in batches until smooth. Return it to the pan and stir over a high heat until heated through. For the minted yoghurt, simply mix everything together with a pinch of salt. Check the seasoning of the soup and stir in the chopped coriander and basil. Pour it into warmed soup bowls and serve garnished with a good spoonful of the minted yoghurt.

MUSSEL AND SAFFRON SOUP

I know this has been done before but it's too good not to give you my version. You need two things for success here – good fat mussels and real saffron stamens – funny, that! In previous versions I've liquidized this soup, but here the mussels have been left whole so that you can appreciate their lovely texture. However, if your mussels are a bit below par, then liquidizing them is probably the best option. Use enough saffron to give the soup a nice colour, but not so much that you can't taste anything else.

Serves 6

1.5 kg (3 lb) fresh mussels
600 ml (1 pint) dry white wine
50 g (2 oz) butter
2 leeks, cleaned and finely chopped
2 sticks celery, finely chopped

1 carrot, peeled and finely chopped
2 cloves garlic, finely chopped
a good pinch of saffron stamens
600 ml (1 pint) double cream
cayenne pepper
Maldon salt
2 tablespoons finely chopped fresh chives

Scrub the mussels well, scrape off any barnacles and pull out the beards protruding from between the two closed shells. Discard any that won't close when they are lightly tapped on the work surface.

Heat a large pan over a high heat. Bung in the mussels and the white wine, cover and cook, shaking the pan every now and then, for 3–4 minutes or until the mussels have opened. Discard any that stay closed.

Tip the mussels into a colander set over a large bowl or another pan and then pass the cooking liquor once more through a chinois or very fine sieve and reserve it. Set aside half of the mussels and remove the meats from the remainder.

Melt the butter in the pan you used for the mussels, add the chopped vegetables and the garlic and cook over a medium–high heat for a few minutes until the vegetables are tender. Add the reserved mussel liquor (except for the last spoonful or two which might contain some sand) and the saffron and leave to simmer for 10 minutes.

Add the cream and bring the soup back to the boil. Add the mussel meats and mussels in their shells, cayenne pepper and a little salt if needed and simmer for about a minute until the mussels have heated through. Stir in the chopped chives, spoon the soup into warmed bowls and serve straight away.

PARTAN BREE

'Partan' is a traditional Scottish name for crab and 'bree' means gravy. So this is 'crab gravy', a name that doesn't do this gorgeous soup justice. Using rice to thicken the soup was a big thing in Victorian times and it is still good. When buying crabs, look for a big, heavy monster which will mean less work for more meat. Failing that, you could use frozen or pasteurized crabmeat but you won't get the same intensity of flavour as using fresh.

Serves 6

1 x 1.75 kg (4 lb) cooked brown crab
600 ml (1 pint) Chicken Stock (see page 181)
50 g (2 oz) long-grain rice
600 ml (1 pint) full cream milk
1 teaspoon anchovy essence

8 drops of Tabasco sauce
Maldon salt and freshly ground white pepper
450 ml (15 fl oz) single cream
a pinch of ground mace
cayenne pepper and chopped fresh chives,
   to garnish

Remove both the brown and white meat from the crab, setting aside the larger pieces of white meat from the claws for garnishing the soup. Put all the pieces of crab shell into a pan with the chicken stock, bring to the boil and leave to simmer for 15 minutes. Meanwhile, put the rice and the milk into another pan, bring to the boil and simmer for 15–20 minutes until the rice is tender.

Strain the crab-flavoured stock through a muslin-lined sieve into another pan. Stir all the crabmeat except the claw meat (you should have about 450 g (1 lb)) into the rice and milk mixture and liquidize until smooth. Then stir this into the pan containing the stock, together with the anchovy essence, Tabasco and some seasoning to taste. Bring gently up to the boil, stir in the cream and the mace and leave until not quite boiling.

Spoon the soup into warmed bowls and garnish with the reserved claw meat, a sprinkling of cayenne pepper and a few chopped chives.

SPICY BUTTERNUT SQUASH SOUP

with coconut milk and coriander

The flavour idea comes from Thai cooking, where spicy flavours are partnered with sweetness (here the chillies with the squash and coconut milk) and often cut with the acidity of lime, ginger and lemon grass. The secret is in the balance, with no one element dominating, so make sure you taste as you go. It's important to find nice ripe squash – not as easy as it sounds since the hard shells prevent you from feeling how squidgy the inside is – so it's best to make friends with a greengrocer in the know.

Serves 6

2 tablespoons groundnut or sunflower oil

1 onion, chopped

900 g (2 lb) butternut squash

900 ml (1½ pints) Chicken Stock (see page 181) or Marinated Vegetable Stock (see page 179)

400 ml (14 fl oz) can coconut milk

3 tablespoons chopped fresh coriander

juice of 1 lime (about 2 tablespoons)

For the red curry paste:

2 cloves garlic

5 cm (2 inch) piece root ginger, peeled and chopped

2–3 long, thin red chillies (depending on how hot you like things), seeded and chopped

1 stalk of lemon grass, outer leaves removed and the core chopped

1 teaspoon ground coriander

1 teaspoon turmeric powder

finely grated zest of 1 lime

1 tablespoon chopped fresh coriander

First make the red curry paste. Simply put all the ingredients into a food processor and blend to a smooth paste.

For the soup, heat the oil in a large pan. Add the onion and fry gently for about 10 minutes until it is very soft and nicely browned. Meanwhile, halve and then peel the butternut squash, scoop out the seeds and cut the flesh into small chunks.

Add the curry paste to the onions and fry, stirring now and then, for 2 minutes. Add the pieces of squash to the pan with the chicken or vegetable stock and simmer for 30 minutes until the squash is nice and tender.

Liquidize the soup (in batches if necessary) until smooth. Return it to the pan, stir in the coconut milk and leave to simmer gently for a further 5 minutes. Add the coriander and lime juice and stir for just 1 minute. Ladle into warmed soup bowls and serve straight away.

RAGOUT OF HEBRIDEAN SHELLFISH

This recipe is a bit cheffy, not to mention expensive, but if you want a 'meaty' soup dish to die for, it's this. You do need seriously fresh, quality shellfish and the optional caviar for maximum impact. So, OK, prepare to sell your soul, put the kids out to work and get on down to a good fishmonger. Having made this investment, don't blow it by overcooking the shellfish. They really need only 2 minutes to cook.

Serves 4

12 langoustine tails
1 small lobster tail
900 g (2 lb) large fresh mussels
175 ml (6 fl oz) dry white wine
175 ml (6 fl oz) dry vermouth
300 ml (10 fl oz) Fish Stock (see page 180)
300 ml (10 fl oz) double cream
a squeeze of fresh lemon juice
Maldon salt and freshly ground white pepper
6 large scallops, cleaned
2 tablespoons caviar (optional)
sprigs of fresh chervil, to garnish

Drop the langoustine and lobster tails into a pan of boiling water, bring back to the boil and then drain. When the tails are cool enough to handle, break open the shells and remove the meats. Cut the lobster meat into 4 neat pieces.

Scrub the mussels well, scrape off any barnacles and pull out the beards protruding from between the two closed shells. Discard any that won't close when they are lightly tapped on the work surface.

Place the mussels in a large pan with the white wine, cover and cook over a high heat for 3–4 minutes until they have opened. Discard any that don't open. Tip the mussels into a colander set over a bowl to collect the cooking liquor. Set aside 12 of the nicest-looking mussels for the garnish and remove the meats from the remainder.

Pour the vermouth into a medium-sized pan and leave it to boil rapidly until it has reduced to about 2 tablespoons. Add the fish stock and all but the last tablespoon of the mussel cooking liquor (which might contain some sand) and boil until reduced by three-quarters. Add the cream and bring back to the boil. Taste the sauce and season with a little lemon juice, salt and pepper.

Cut the scallops in half and add them to the sauce with the langoustine, lobster and mussel meats. Bring the sauce up to a gentle simmer and cook for 1–2 minutes. Lift the shellfish out of the sauce and arrange them attractively in the centre of 4 warmed serving bowls. Take the sauce off the heat and stir in the caviar, if using. Spoon the sauce over the shellfish and garnish with the reserved mussels and the sprigs of fresh chervil.

CULLEN SKINK

(smoked haddock, potato and chive soup)

Another traditional Scottish soup and one that's stood the test of time. It's vital to use top-quality undyed smoked haddock to get the true flavour. The stuff from R. & R. Spink in Arbroath is the best I've tasted and I believe they now supply some of the big supermarkets, so go for it.

Serves 4-6

350 g (12 oz) floury potatoes, such as
  Maris Piper or King Edward, peeled and
  cut into chunks
50 g (2 oz) butter
1 onion, chopped

450 g (1 lb) Finnan smoked haddock fillets
300 ml (10 fl oz) water
Maldon salt and freshly ground black pepper
600 ml (1 pint) milk
1 tablespoon chopped fresh chives
4 tablespoons double cream

Cook the potatoes in lightly salted boiling water for 20 minutes. Meanwhile, melt half the butter in a large pan. Add the onion and cook it gently for about 7 minutes until it is soft but not browned. Cut the smoked haddock fillets into large pieces and add them and the water to the onions. Bring up to a simmer, cover and leave to cook for 10 minutes until the fish is just cooked through. Lift the fish onto a plate and, when it is cool enough to handle, break it into large flakes, discarding any skin and bones. Reserve the cooking liquor.

Drain the potatoes and mash them until smooth. Now press them through a sieve – this will give an even smoother finish to the soup – and beat in the rest of the butter and some salt and pepper.

Whisk the mashed potato into the cooking liquor until the texture is smooth and creamy and then stir in the milk. Bring up to a simmer, cover and leave to cook for 3–4 minutes. Stir in the flaked fish, chives and cream and season to taste with a little more salt and pepper if necessary.

KIDNEY SOUP

When I was a wee boy, tinned kidney soup (Grannie's, I think) and hot buttered toast were a treat on coming home from school that I've never forgotten, and this recipe attempts to try and recapture that taste. Unlike most of my soup recipes, this one needs good stock, preferably home-made or the ready-made supermarket stuff, but not cubes.

Serves 6

350 g (12 oz) lambs' kidneys
3 tablespoons sunflower oil
2 small sticks celery, finely chopped
2 medium onions, finely chopped
2 carrots, peeled and finely chopped
40 g (1½ oz) plain flour
1.75 litres (3 pints) good lamb or Beef Stock
   (see page 182)

1½ tablespoons tomato purée
2 fresh bay leaves
2 sprigs of fresh thyme
Maldon salt and freshly ground white pepper
3 small medium-thick slices white bread, crusts
   removed
3 tablespoons Clarified Butter (see page 183),
   warmed
1 tablespoon chopped fresh parsley

Halve the kidneys and snip out the cores with scissors. Set aside 4 of the halves and finely chop the rest. Heat the oil in a large pan, add the celery, onions and carrots and cook over a medium heat for 10 minutes until soft and lightly browned. Add the chopped kidney and fry for 2–3 minutes, then lower the heat, stir in the flour and cook for 1 minute. Take the pan off the heat and gradually stir in the stock. Stir in the tomato purée, bay leaves, thyme sprigs and some seasoning and bring to the boil, stirring. Cover and leave to simmer for 30 minutes.

Meanwhile, preheat the oven to 200°C/400°F/Gas Mark 6. Cut the bread into 1 cm (½ inch) cubes and toss them with half of the warm clarified butter. Spread them out onto a tray and bake them in the oven for 5–7 minutes until crisp and lightly browned. Remove from the oven and set aside.

Remove the bay leaves and thyme sprigs from the soup and liquidize a quarter of it (about 450 ml/15 fl oz) until smooth. Return this to the pan containing the rest of the soup and bring back to a gentle simmer. Fry the reserved kidney slices in the rest of the clarified butter for about 1 minute on each side until they are lightly browned and just cooked. Lift them onto a chopping board and cut them into small, neat dice. Taste the soup for seasoning and serve in warmed bowls sprinkled with the diced kidneys, croûtons and chopped parsley.

The cold, deep, clear waters

around Scotland's rugged coastline

yield are, without doubt, our richest

harvest: fish and shellfish of an

almost unbelievable quality.

STARTERS

SEARED SCALLOP FILO TARTLETS

with basil, tomato and caramelized onion

Not really tarts – the crispy filo discs just provide a nice crispy base for the sweet, seared scallops and the rather delicious tomato, basil and onion dressing. Do use scallops that haven't been soaked in water to plump them up and make them taste of – well, water. Frozen ones are just as bad. Big, 'hand-dived' scallops are what you want every time. If cash is tight, halve the number of scallops that you use and double the amount of dressing, rather than waste money on the larger quantity of dud scallops.

Serves 4

10 large sheets of filo pastry
olive oil
2 large onions, thinly sliced
6 plum tomatoes

4 tablespoons lemon juice
15 g (½ oz) fresh basil leaves, torn into small
  pieces
Maldon salt and freshly ground white pepper
8 large scallops, cleaned
1 tablespoon balsamic or red wine vinegar

Preheat the oven to 180°C/350°F/Gas Mark 4. Stack up the sheets of pastry and cut out four 15 cm (6 inch) circles using an upturned bowl as a template. Separate them into individual discs, brush each one with a little of the oil and lay them out in pairs, one disc on top of another, giving them some wrinkles so that a more attractive finish is achieved. Place on a baking sheet a few at a time and bake for 8–10 minutes until crisp and golden. You should end up with 20 double-thickness discs of pastry. Remove and leave to cool. These can be made hours or even days in advance and kept in an airtight tin if you wish.

Heat 4 tablespoons of oil in a pan. Add the onions and cook over quite a high heat, stirring frequently, until they are soft and nicely caramelized. Meanwhile, skin the tomatoes – with a blowtorch or with boiling water – then seed them and cut them into very neat dice. Mix them with 3 tablespoons of oil, 1 tablespoon of the lemon juice, the basil and some seasoning. Set aside.

Pat the scallops dry with some kitchen paper. Detach the corals (roes) and save them for another dish. Cut each white scallop meat into 3 discs. Heat a large frying pan until it is quite hot. Add 2 tablespoons of oil and the scallop slices and sear over a high heat for 1 minute on one side only until richly browned and crispy. The slight rawness of the uncooked side will give them an excellent, sensuous texture. Do this in batches if your frying pan is not very large. Remove them to a plate and season with the rest of the lemon juice and some salt and pepper.

Stir the caramelized onions into the tomato and basil mixture with the vinegar. Stack 5 discs of filo pastry on each plate and spoon on the tomato and onion mixture. Overlap 6 scallop slices over the top of each one and serve straight away while the pastry is still crisp.

SALMON SUSHI

With a bit of practice, making sushi isn't that hard. But make sure you've got proper Japanese sushi rice and that you rinse it really well. You can use any kind of fish but it must be very fresh. You can make vegetarian variations too using mango, avocado, cucumber and spring onion. Sushi rolls (illustrated on page 7) can be made up to 24 hours in advance, wrapped in clingfilm and sliced at the last moment.

Serves 6

375 g (13 oz) Japanese sticky rice
600 ml (1 pint) water
2 tablespoons caster sugar
1 teaspoon Maldon salt
4 tablespoons rice vinegar
5 sheets of dried nori seaweed
175 g (6 oz) thin salmon fillet, skinned and cut
  into long thin strips

3 teaspoons wasabi paste or powder, plus
  extra to serve
15 fresh chives, cut into long pieces

To serve:
2 tablespoons Japanese pickled ginger juice
4 tablespoons Japanese soy sauce
25 g (1 oz) Japanese pickled ginger

Put the rice into a sieve and wash it under running cold water, working your fingers through the grains until the water runs clear. Drain the rice and put it into a pan with 600 ml (1 pint) water. Bring quickly to the boil, then turn the heat down low and cook for 10 minutes. Remove from the heat, cover and leave undisturbed for 10 minutes. This timing is crucial to produce the correct consistency for the sushi.

Stir the sugar and salt into the vinegar until dissolved. Turn the rice out into a bowl and stir the vinegar mixture into it, fanning the rice as you do so to cool it and produce a sheen.

For sushi rolls, place a sheet of seaweed on a sushi mat (see page 10). Spread two-thirds of it with a 7 mm (⅓ inch) thick layer of the rice, leaving a clear strip down one long edge. Lay a strip of the salmon lengthways down the centre of the rice and spread it with a little of the wasabi. If you are using wasabi powder, first mix it to a smooth paste with a little cold water. Add a few chives, then dampen the clean edge of the seaweed sheet with a little water. Using the mat to help you, lift up one long edge and roll the seaweed into shape, sealing it into a secure roll with the dampened edge. Cut the roll across into 2 cm (¾ inch) lengths. Repeat with the remaining sheets of seaweed. Cut one end of some rolls at an angle if you wish.

To present the sushi, mix the pickled ginger juice with the soy sauce and pour it into a small dipping saucer. Arrange a small pile of pickled ginger, a teaspoon of wasabi paste, the sushi and the saucer of sauce on a large plate and serve.

SALMON NIÇOISE TARTLETS

A twist on a classic combination of ingredients, these tartlets not only taste great but look stunning with all the different colours showing through the egg. You can make the cases up to 24 hours in advance, and the raw pastry cases can be frozen for up to 3 weeks. Prepare the bits and pieces for the filling in advance and pour on the egg mix just before baking. The tartlets are great on their own or with a few dressed salad leaves.

Serves 6

100 g (4 oz) skinned salmon fillet
Maldon salt and freshly ground black pepper
50 g (2 oz) French beans, topped and tailed
12 small cherry tomatoes
100 g (4 oz) cooked small new potatoes
12 pitted black olives
2 tablespoons chopped fresh basil
2 farm-fresh eggs
175 ml (6 fl oz) double cream

2 teaspoons balsamic vinegar
2 tablespoons finely grated Parmesan

For the pastry:
275 g (10 oz) plain flour
a pinch of Maldon salt
65 g (2½ oz) chilled butter, diced
65 g (2½ oz) chilled lard or vegetable
  shortening, diced
1½ tablespoons very cold water
1 medium farm-fresh egg white

For the tartlet cases, sift the flour and salt into a food processor and add the butter and lard. Process until the mixture looks like fine breadcrumbs. Transfer to a bowl and stir in the water until the mixture starts to stick together in small lumps. Gently bring it together into a ball and knead once or twice on a lightly floured surface until smooth. Divide the pastry into 4 pieces and use to line four loose-bottomed tartlet tins 11 cm (4½ inch) wide × 4 cm (1½ inch) deep. Slide them into the fridge and leave them to chill for 20 minutes.

Preheat the oven to 200°C/400°F/Gas Mark 6. Line the pastry cases with crumpled pieces of greaseproof paper (for a better fit) and baking beans and bake for 11 minutes. Remove the paper and beans and bake the cases for another 6–9 minutes. Now brush the base of each case with a little of the unbeaten egg white and return them to the oven for 1 minute. Remove them from the oven and set aside.

To prepare the filling, cut the salmon into 2 cm (¾ inch) strips and season with a little salt and pepper. Cut the beans into 2.5 cm (1 inch) pieces and blanch them in boiling salted water for 2 minutes. Drain and refresh under cold water. Cover the cherry tomatoes with boiling water, leave for a few seconds, then drain and cover with cold water. Peel off the skins. Cut the new potatoes and olives lengthways into quarters.

Arrange the salmon, beans, tomatoes, potatoes, olives and basil in each tartlet case so that all the bits are visible and stick out above the rim of the pastry case. This will help to give the finished tarts an attractive appearance. Mix the eggs with the double cream, balsamic vinegar, Parmesan and a little seasoning. Pour the mixture over the filling and bake in the oven for about 20 minutes or until they are just set in the centre and lightly browned. Carefully lift the tartlets out of the tins and serve while they are still warm.

BUTTERFLIED LANGOUSTINES

with baby bok choi

Chilli and black bean sauce is found in most Chinese supermarkets and there seem to be a hundred different varieties available. Only experimenting will tell you which is best; my favourite is the Mong Lee Shang brand. You really need fresh (that means alive!) langoustines, but you could use raw tiger prawns instead. It's just that langoustines have such an incredible flavour. Be careful not to overcook them – always err on the side of underdone or you lose the texture, which should be yielding not rubbery.

Serves 4

20 uncooked langoustines or large
   whole prawns
3 tablespoons good-quality dark soy sauce
1 tablespoon clear honey
1 tablespoon Dijon mustard

2 tablespoons freshly squeezed lemon juice
5 tablespoons sunflower oil
350 g (12 oz) baby bok choi, trimmed
1 tablespoon chilli and black bean sauce
2 tablespoons roughly chopped fresh
   coriander
Maldon salt and freshly ground black pepper

Butterfly the langoustines or prawns by cutting them in half lengthways through the shell, keeping them attached at the tail end. Mix the soy sauce with the honey, mustard and 1 tablespoon of lemon juice. Pour into a shallow dish, toss in the shellfish and marinate for 1 hour.

Preheat a barbecue or grill to medium–high. Cook the langoustines or prawns for 3–4 minutes, turning them over half-way through. At the same time, heat the oil in a large pan. Add the bok choi and stir-fry over a high heat for 1–2 minutes. Add the rest of the lemon juice, the chilli and black bean sauce, coriander and seasoning and toss together well.

To serve, pile the bok choi into the centres of 4 warmed plates and arrange the langoustines or prawns around it.

ARBROATH SMOKIE CROQUETTES
with a spicy tomato salsa and balsamic vinegar syrup

You might not think that croquettes are very sexy, but the big flavour of the smokies and the spiciness of the salsa make this into a dish worthy of its own star billing. The croquettes can be frozen once breaded. Just defrost them overnight in the fridge on some kitchen paper. The Balsamic Vinegar Syrup (extravagant, but worth it) keeps for months in a sealed bottle.

Serves 6

750 g (1½ lb) floury main crop potatoes, such
  as King Edward or Maris Piper
15 g (½ oz) butter
900 g (2 lb) Arbroath smokies
1–2 tablespoons double cream
Maldon salt and freshly ground white pepper
sunflower oil for deep frying
25 g (1 oz) plain flour, seasoned with
  ½ teaspoon Maldon salt and some pepper
1 medium farm-fresh egg, beaten

75 g (3 oz) fresh white breadcrumbs
Balsamic Vinegar Syrup, to serve
  (see page 183)

For the spicy tomato salsa:
6 small vine tomatoes, skinned and seeded
1 small red onion, peeled and quartered
1 long, thin red chilli
1 large clove garlic, cut into slivers
2 teaspoons lemon juice
a handful of fresh coriander leaves
2 tablespoons olive oil

For the croquettes, peel the potatoes and cut them into chunks. Cook in boiling salted water until tender. Drain well, tip back into the pan and mash with the butter until smooth. Press through a sieve with a wooden spoon to make a very smooth purée and leave to cool a little bit. Meanwhile, skin and bone the Arbroath smokies and break the flesh into small pieces. You should be left with about 350 g (12 oz) of flaked fish. Add the flaked fish, cream and a little salt and pepper to the potatoes and mix well. Divide the mixture into 12 and form into barrel shapes. Place on a baking tray, cover with clingfilm and chill for 20 minutes.

For the salsa, cut the tomatoes into arc shapes, cut the onion lengthways into thin slices and cut the chilli across into thin slices (removing the seeds if you wish). Put them all in a bowl with the garlic and stir in the lemon juice and some seasoning. Cover and chill.

Pour some oil into a pan until it is about one-third full and heat it to 180°C/350°F. Dip the croquettes into the seasoned flour, the egg and then the breadcrumbs, pressing the breadcrumbs on well to give a thick, even coating. Cook the croquettes, 4 at a time, for about 4 minutes until crisp and golden. Lift each batch out onto some kitchen paper and keep warm in a low oven. Stir the coriander leaves and olive oil into the salsa. Place 1 or 2 croquettes on each plate and pile the spicy tomato salsa alongside. Drizzle a little of the balsamic vinegar syrup around the edge of each plate and serve while the croquettes are still hot and crunchy.

BAKED PRAWN SOUFFLÉS

with a saffron mayonnaise

This might seem like a waste of good tiger prawns – but wait until you taste these light, little fishy clouds with the saffron mayonnaise melting into them to form a liquid centre. Actually, the Chinese quite often mince prawns for making things such as prawn toasts and prawn balls, so I feel vindicated in turning them into soufflés.

Serves 6

15 g (½ oz) butter

25 g (1 oz) fresh white breadcrumbs

15 g (½ oz) Parmesan, finely grated

175 g (6 oz) raw peeled tiger prawns

2 farm-fresh egg yolks

Maldon salt

¼ teaspoon cayenne pepper

150 ml (5 fl oz) double cream

4 farm-fresh egg whites

½ teaspoon freshly squeezed lemon juice

For the saffron mayonnaise:

a pinch of saffron stamens

1 farm-fresh egg yolk

1 teaspoon lemon juice

¼ teaspoon Maldon salt

150 ml (5 fl oz) olive oil

150 ml (5 fl oz) sunflower oil

a few drops of Tabasco sauce

For the mayonnaise, put the saffron stamens into a pestle and mortar and grind to a fine powder. Tip the powder into a small bowl (use a pastry brush to make sure you get all the powder out), add the egg yolk, lemon juice and salt and whisk together well. Now very gradually whisk in the oils until the finished mixture is thick and silky smooth. Whisk in the Tabasco and a little more lemon juice to taste if you wish. Cover with some clingfilm and chill until needed.

For the shellfish soufflés, all the ingredients must be very cold before you start. Slide a baking sheet onto the middle shelf of the oven and preheat it to 220°C/425°F/Gas Mark 7. Generously grease six 7.5 cm (3 inch) ramekins with the butter. Mix the breadcrumbs with the Parmesan and shake some around in each ramekin until the base and sides are well coated.

Put the raw prawns into a food processor and blend for a few seconds. Add the egg yolks, ½ teaspoon salt and the cayenne pepper and blitz once more until smooth. Add the cream and blend for no more than 10 seconds. Scrape the mixture into a large bowl. In another large bowl, whisk the egg whites with a good pinch of salt and the lemon juice until they form stiff peaks. Gently fold one large spoonful of the egg whites into the prawn mixture and then gently fold in the remainder.

Spoon the mixture into the ramekins and slide them onto the baking sheet. Bake for about 10–12 minutes until risen and golden brown. Make a small slit in the top of each one, drop in a teaspoonful of the saffron mayonnaise and serve immediately.

RAZOR CLAM RISOTTO

with peas, bacon and mint

This unlikely sounding dish works really well as the sweetness of the clams and peas matches the saltiness of the bacon and Parmesan, and the mint adds a nice clean flavour. You could use scallops or langoustines instead of razor clams, which can be a tad difficult to find. In fact, the risotto is fabby enough to be served on its own. As always with risotto, use the best arborio rice and Parmesan available. The stock, however, is just dandy made from a good-quality cube.

Serves 4

750 g (1½ lb) razor clams, scrubbed clean
350 ml (12 fl oz) dry white wine
about 900 ml (1½ pints) Chicken Stock (see page 181)
75 ml (3 fl oz) olive oil
4 rashers rindless streaky bacon, chopped
1 onion, finely chopped

1 clove garlic, finely chopped
225 g (8 oz) arborio rice
100 g (4 oz) peas, fresh or frozen
50 g (2 oz) butter
25 g (1 oz) Parmesan, finely grated, plus extra to serve (optional)
2 tablespoons chopped fresh mint, plus extra to serve (optional)
Maldon salt and freshly ground white pepper

Place the razor clams and 150 ml (5 fl oz) of the white wine in a large pan. Cover and cook over a high heat for a few minutes until the clams have opened. Discard any that remain closed. Tip them into a colander set over another bowl and, when they are cool enough to handle, remove the meats from the shells and cut them into fine dice. Pour all but the last tablespoon of the cooking liquid (which might contain some sand) into a measuring jug and make up to 900 ml (1½ pints) with the chicken stock.

Heat the olive oil in a large pan. Add the bacon, onion and garlic and stir-fry over a medium heat until the bacon has lightly browned and the onion has become translucent. Add the rice and stir it around for a couple of minutes until it has become well coated in the oil. Add the rest of the white wine and simmer for another 4–5 minutes, stirring, until almost all the liquid been absorbed by the rice. Now lob in half the stock and bring up to the boil, stirring. Reduce the heat to a simmer and leave the risotto to cook until the stock has been absorbed. Add the rest of the stock and continue to cook, stirring occasionally, until the rice is tender but with a little bite left in it, and the texture is rich and creamy. This should take about 20 minutes in all.

Now add the peas and stir them into the risotto with the butter, Parmesan, diced razor clams and mint. Season to taste with salt and pepper and cook for 2 minutes. Spoon into 4 warmed serving bowls and sprinkle with a little more cheese and a bit more chopped mint if you wish.

Mussels

One of the things that I keep banging on about is to remember that recipes are just guidelines and in most cases are to be mucked about with or personalized. So the next four recipes are a variation on a theme, that good old bistro staple, moules à la marinière.

STEAMED MUSSELS

with chilli, red onion, tomato and basil

In this first version the flavouring comes from the southern Mediterranean, so you get lovely tomato, garlic and basil flavours with the heat of the chilli spicing things up.

**Serves 4
(or 2 as a main course)**

900 g (2 lb) fresh mussels

2 tablespoons extra virgin olive oil, plus a little
   extra to serve

2 cloves garlic, very finely chopped

½ medium red onion, very finely chopped

1 finely chopped long, thin red chilli, seeds left
   in if you like things hot

50 ml (2 fl oz) dry white wine

4 well-flavoured tomatoes, skinned, seeded
   and chopped

4 tablespoons chopped fresh basil

freshly ground black pepper

2 teaspoons lemon juice

Maldon salt

a loaf of fresh ciabatta, to serve

Scrub the mussels well, scrape off any barnacles and pull out the beards protruding from between the two closed shells. Discard any that won't close when they are lightly tapped on the work surface.

Put the olive oil, garlic, onion and chilli into a large pan and cook over a gentle heat for 5 minutes until the onion is just soft. Add the white wine, chopped tomatoes and the mussels, then cover and cook over a high heat, giving the pan a good shake every now and then, for 3–4 minutes until the mussels have opened.

Uncover the pan and discard any mussels that are still closed. Add the basil and plenty of freshly ground black pepper, then taste the sauce and add the lemon juice and a little more salt if necessary. Turn the mussels over once or twice to distribute the basil evenly and then spoon them into large, warmed soup plates. Drizzle over a little more olive oil and serve with chunks of ciabatta bread.

STEAMED MUSSELS

with a lemon, cream and parsley sauce

This version is closer to the original but the cream makes it richer and the lemon zest gives it a fabby tang – I'm dribbling now!

Serves 4
(or 2 as a main course)

900 g (2 lb) fresh mussels
25 g (1 oz) butter
4 large shallots, peeled and very
  finely chopped
1 clove garlic, very finely chopped

50 ml (2 fl oz) dry white wine
150 ml (5 fl oz) double cream
finely grated zest of ½ small lemon
3 tablespoons chopped fresh flatleaf parsley
1 tablespoon lemon juice
Maldon salt and freshly ground black pepper
crusty French bread, to serve

Scrub the mussels well, scrape off any barnacles and pull out the beards protruding from between the two closed shells. Discard any that won't close when they are lightly tapped on the work surface.

Melt the butter in a large pan. Add the shallots and garlic and cook gently for about 3 minutes. Add the wine and the mussels, cover and cook over a high heat, shaking the pan every now and then, until the mussels have opened. Discard any that remain closed.

Remove the pan from the heat and lift the mussels out with a slotted spoon into a large bowl. Keep them warm. Return the pan to the heat and boil the remaining cooking liquor rapidly for 6 minutes until reduced and well flavoured. Add the cream and the lemon zest and continue to boil for 4 minutes, stirring all the time to prevent the sauce from sticking, during which time it will thicken slightly. Add the chopped parsley and some lemon juice, salt and pepper to taste. Return the mussels to the pan and turn over in the sauce for a minute or two until heated through. Spoon into large, warmed soup plates and serve with chunks of crusty French bread.

STEAMED MUSSELS

with chilli and black bean sauce

Off to the Orient for inspiration here. The results of this recipe should be fresh and fragrant flavours with the ginger, spring onions and soy all doing their thing together. Make sure you use light sesame oil, and if you wanted you could sprinkle over some toasted sesame seeds at the end and serve with some cooked noodles. Yum!

Serves 4
(or 2 as a main course)

900 g (2 lb) fresh mussels
4 spring onions, trimmed
1 tablespoon groundnut or sunflower oil
2 teaspoons sesame oil, plus extra for serving
1 clove garlic, very finely chopped

1 cm (½ inch) piece fresh root ginger, peeled and finely chopped
1 tablespoon chilli and black bean sauce
2 tablespoons rice wine vinegar mixed with 2 teaspoons caster sugar
1 tablespoon dark soy sauce
2 tablespoons roughly chopped fresh coriander

Scrub the mussels well, scrape off any barnacles and pull out the beards protruding from between the two closed shells. Discard any that won't close when they are lightly tapped on the work surface.

Cut the green tops off each spring onion and slice them into long, fine shreds. Thinly slice the remaining white parts. Heat the groundnut oil and 2 teaspoons of sesame oil in a large pan. Add the white parts of the spring onions, the garlic and ginger and stir-fry for 2–3 minutes. Add the chilli and black bean sauce, the mussels, rice wine vinegar dressing and soy sauce. Cover and cook over a high heat for 3–4 minutes, shaking the pan every now and then, until the mussels have opened. Discard any that remain closed.

Add the chopped coriander and most of the shredded green tops of the spring onions to the pan and turn everything over once or twice. Ladle the mussels into warmed bowls, drizzle over a little more sesame oil and serve sprinkled with the remaining spring onion shreds. If you are serving this with cooked noodles, remove the mussels from the pan with a slotted spoon after you have added the coriander and spring onion tops, and add the noodles to the sauce. Warm them through, divide them among the bowls and then spoon the mussels on top.

STEAMED MUSSELS

with garam masala, coconut milk and basil

Thailand is the source of the sweet-spicy-tangy flavour sensation in this recipe. Get the balance right here and you're in food heaven.

Serves 4
(or 2 as a main course)

900 g (2 lb) fresh mussels
1 tablespoon groundnut or sunflower oil
2 cloves garlic, finely chopped
1 cm (½ inch) piece fresh root ginger, peeled
   and finely chopped
1 stalk of lemon grass, outer leaves removed
   and the tender core finely chopped

1 chopped long, thin red chilli, seeds left in
   if you like things hot
2 teaspoons garam masala
1 tablespoon Thai fish sauce
2 teaspoons palm or light muscovado sugar
2 tablespoons lime juice
120 ml (4 fl oz) coconut milk
2 tablespoons fresh basil, very finely shredded
1 tablespoon chopped fresh coriander

Scrub the mussels well, scrape off any barnacles and pull out the beards protruding from between the two closed shells. Discard any that won't close when they are lightly tapped on the work surface.

Heat the oil in a large pan. Add the garlic, ginger, lemon grass, chilli and garam masala and fry for 3–4 minutes. Add the fish sauce, sugar, lime juice and coconut milk, bring up to the boil and reduce for 3 minutes. Add the mussels, cover and cook over a high heat for 3–4 minutes until they have opened. Discard any that remain closed.

Add the basil and coriander to the pan and turn over the mussels once or twice. Ladle them into hot bowls and serve straight away.

NETTLE PASTA

with a cockle vinaigrette

I'm rather proud of this here dish, as it was made up on the spur of the moment during the filming of the TV series. Sometimes the best ideas come when your back is up against the wall, which is just what happened to your intrepid chef when he realized – too late – that he had planned to film a dish containing cockles, which he had never cooked before. Silly boy! However, desperation produced this and it was pronounced a winner (by me and the rest of the crew at least). There you go, just because you're on the telly doesn't mean you always know what you're doing!

Serves 4

4 good (gloved) handfuls of nettle tips
275 g (10 oz) plain flour
2 medium farm-fresh eggs
2 medium farm-fresh egg yolks

For the cockle vinaigrette:
1.75 kg (3 lb) cockles in their shells,
    scrubbed clean
4 tablespoons red wine

3 shallots, finely chopped
1 clove garlic, finely chopped
6 tablespoons olive oil
3 tablespoons chopped mixed fresh basil,
    coriander and chives
Tomatoes Concassées (see page 184),
    use 4 tomatoes
1½ tablespoons Cabernet Sauvignon or
    another good-quality red wine vinegar
freshly ground white pepper
15 g (½ oz) butter

For the pasta, drop the nettle tips into a pan of well-salted boiling water, drain immediately and refresh under cold water. Squeeze dry by hand or in a clean tea towel. Put the flour into a food processor, turn on the machine and then add the eggs, egg yolks and nettles through the lid. Whizz for 2–3 minutes until the mixture looks like fine breadcrumbs (it shouldn't be dusty, nor should it be a big, gooey ball). Tip the mixture out onto a work surface, form into a ball and knead for 1 minute. Wrap the dough in clingfilm and chill for 1 hour if you have time.

Cut the chilled dough in half. Flatten each piece with a rolling pin to a 5 mm (¼ inch) thickness, fold it over and roll it out, refolding and rolling it 7 times until you have a 7.5 × 18 cm (3 × 7 inch) rectangle. It is important to work the dough until it is nice and shiny as this gives it a good texture.

If you have a pasta machine, start with it at its widest setting and pass the dough through the rollers. Repeat this process, decreasing the roller setting each time you pass the dough through until you reach the penultimate setting. Pass the dough through once more at this setting and then

leave it to dry for 5 minutes. Finally, set the machine on its finest cutters (for spaghetti) and pass the dough through. If you do not have a pasta machine, simply roll out the pasta on a floured work surface with a rolling pin until you have a 3 mm (⅛ inch) thickness. Roll the sheet of pasta carefully into a cylinder and cut this into thin strips with a sharp knife to give you spaghetti. Unroll each slice into a strand as you cut, otherwise the pasta will stick together. Drop the pasta straight away into a large pan of boiling salted water, bring it back to the boil and cook for 2½ minutes. Drain the pasta, drop it into a bowl of cold water to stop it cooking, then drain once more and set aside.

For the cockle vinaigrette, soak the cockles in several changes of water to ensure that all the sand has come out of them. Discard any that won't open when given a sharp tap. Place them in a large pan with the red wine, cover and cook over a high heat, giving the pan a good shake every now and then, for 4–5 minutes, until they have opened. Discard any that remain closed. Tip into a colander set over a bowl to collect the cooking liquor. Pour all but the last tablespoon of the liquor (which might contain some sand) back into a clean pan and add the chopped shallots and garlic. Leave to simmer for 10 minutes until the liquor has reduced to about 6 tablespoons and the shallots have softened. Add the oil and leave it to infuse over a low heat for 5 minutes.

Meanwhile, remove the cockles from their shells. Add them to the shallot mixture with the chopped herbs, tomatoes, vinegar and some freshly ground white pepper (but no salt). Place the butter and 2 tablespoons of water in a large pan. As soon as the butter has melted and the water is simmering, add the pasta and toss it around every now and then until it has heated through. Twirl each portion of the pasta onto a large roasting fork and then lift each 'tower' into the centre of each serving bowl. Spoon around the cockle vinaigrette and serve immediately.

PEPPERED TUNA CARPACCIO

with a spicy lentil salad in a soy vinaigrette

Some people are a bit funny about eating raw fish, which is fair enough: I hate tripe! So if you are such a person, move onto another recipe because this is essentially raw fish. It's got a lovely spicy crust and the lentil salad lends some earthy texture, but it's still nice, shiny, raw tuna – yum!

Serves 6

2 tablespoons dark soy sauce

1 tablespoon Dijon mustard

1 tablespoon clear honey

2 tablespoons sunflower oil

225 g (8 oz) loin of tuna taken from a large
    fish, well trimmed

2 tablespoons Sichuan peppercorns

1 tablespoon Maldon salt

a good pinch of Chinese five-spice powder

sprigs of fresh coriander, to garnish

For the spicy lentil salad:

225 g (8 oz) Puy lentils

2 thin slices fresh root ginger

3 cloves garlic, peeled

1 medium red onion, very finely chopped

1 long, thin red chilli, seeded and very finely
    chopped

3 tablespoons chopped fresh coriander

2 tablespoons rice wine vinegar, or white wine
    vinegar mixed with 1 tablespoon caster sugar

4 tablespoons sunflower oil

1 tablespoon Japanese soy sauce

Mix together the soy sauce, mustard and honey and pour into a small shallow dish. Heat a large frying pan until it is very hot, add the oil, then sear the tuna over a high heat, turning it now and then, until it has cooked all over to a depth of about 5 mm (¼ inch). Transfer the tuna to the soy mixture, turning it occasionally, and leave until cold.

Meanwhile, heat a dry, heavy-based frying pan over a high heat. Add the peppercorns and toss for a few seconds until they darken slightly and start to smell aromatic. Tip them into a mortar and coarsely crush them with the pestle. Stir in the salt and five-spice powder, then sprinkle the mixture onto a plate. Lift the tuna out of the marinade and dip it in the spices so that they form a thin, even coating. Wrap the fish tightly in clingfilm and chill for 24 hours.

For the salad, bring a pan of lightly salted water to the boil. Add the lentils, ginger and a whole clove of garlic and leave them to simmer very gently for 20 minutes until just tender. Do not have the water boiling too vigorously or the lentils will start to fall apart.

Drain the lentils, discarding the ginger and garlic, and leave to cool. Finely chop the remaining garlic and stir it into the lentils with the other salad ingredients. Leave to go cold.

To serve, remove the tuna from the fridge and unwrap it. Slice the loin across into very thin slices using a long, very sharp knife. Spoon the lentils into the centre of each plate, cover with 3–4 slices of the tuna and serve garnished with sprigs of fresh coriander.

BARBECUED MACKEREL KEBABS

with aloo bhaji

So you think mackerel is a bit oily, a cheap fish fit only for bait? Try this and I guarantee you will change your mind! Mackerel loves spices and because it has a bit of extra oil in its flesh it means it doesn't dry out under the intense heat of the barbie. If you can't face barbecuing, then simply sear the kebabs on a ribbed, cast-iron grill pan, but to achieve mackerel nirvana get one of those instant foil-tray barbies and stick it on the back doorstep. The mackerel must be dead fresh – less than 24 hours old – or else you'll have oily old fish fit only for bait! And if you can't be bothered with the aloo bhaji, simply push the kebabs into pitta bread that you've warmed through on the grill, pull out the skewer and enjoy.

Serves 4

2 medium-sized mackerel, filleted and cut into
    2.5 cm (1 inch) pieces
Maldon salt and freshly ground white pepper
dressed salad leaves and big wedges of
    lemon or lime, to serve

For the marinade:
1 long, thin red chilli, finely chopped
    (seeds and all)
2 cloves garlic, finely chopped
finely grated zest of 1 lemon
juice of ½ lemon (about 1½ tablespoons)

1 tablespoon chopped fresh coriander
2–3 tablespoons olive oil

For the aloo bhaji:
350 g (12 oz) potatoes
2–3 tablespoons sunflower oil
½ teaspoon cumin seeds
½ green chilli, seeded and very finely
    chopped
½ teaspoon ground cumin
¼ teaspoon cayenne pepper
¼ teaspoon turmeric powder
¼ teaspoon garam masala

Set up the barbecue before you start preparing the ingredients. This way, the coals will have time to become beautiful red embers that give off the perfect heat for searing the mackerel. If you are using wooden, rather than metal, skewers, this is the time to put them in water to soak so that they don't burn on the barbie and taint the flavour of the fish.

Combine all the marinade ingredients together in a large glass bowl and season. Mix in the fish so that it's completely coated in the marinade and leave to stand for half an hour for the fish to absorb maximum flavour.

Meanwhile, peel the potatoes and cut them into 2.5 cm (1 inch) cubes. Part-cook them in boiling salted water for 7 minutes and then drain well and leave to go cold. Heat the oil in a large frying pan. Add the potatoes and fry them over a medium heat for about 7–10 minutes, turning them over now and then, until they are light golden brown. Sprinkle over the cumin seeds and the chopped green chilli and continue to cook for 3–5 minutes. Then sprinkle over the ground cumin, cayenne pepper and turmeric powder and cook for another 5 minutes, turning the potatoes as they fry so that they get coated in a rich, spicy crust. Sprinkle over the garam masala and some seasoning and toss together well. Keep warm.

Thread the pieces of fish onto the skewers and whack them onto the barbecue for about 5 minutes on the first side. Baste them with a little of the marinade while they are cooking, then turn them and cook for a further couple of minutes. Serve with the aloo bhaji, salad leaves and lemon or lime wedges.

PENNE PASTA

with broccoli and Parmesan

This seems a bit bizarre, I know, but do give it a go because it tastes sublime and has been known to convert ardent broccoli haters into fans. Do use good-quality fresh pasta, preferably made with egg, and definitely not the dried quick-cook variety, which has a horrid texture. Good pasta should work with the sauce and absorb just the right amount.

Serves 4

750 g (1½ lb) broccoli
350–450 g (12 oz–1 lb) fresh penne pasta
120 ml (4 fl oz) extra virgin olive oil

2 large cloves garlic, crushed
1 tablespoon freshly squeezed lemon juice
50 g (2 oz) Parmesan, finely grated
Maldon salt and freshly ground black pepper

Bring two large pans of well-salted water to the boil. Meanwhile, discard the large stalks from the broccoli and cut the green heads into small florets. You want to be left with about 450 g (1 lb). Add the broccoli to one pan, bring back to the boil and cook for 2 minutes. Drain, reserving some of the cooking water and set aside half of the nicest-looking florets. Add the pasta to the second pan and cook for 6–8 minutes, or according to the packet instructions, until *al dente*. Meanwhile, heat half the oil in a large, deep frying pan, add the garlic and the other half of the broccoli florets and fry over a high heat for 2–3 minutes until the florets are lightly browned and quite soft. Tip them into a food processor and add the rest of the olive oil, 6 tablespoons of the reserved broccoli water, the lemon juice, half the Parmesan and plenty of seasoning. Blitz the mixture for a minute or so until really smooth.

Drain the pasta well, return it to the pan with the broccoli sauce and toss together well. Now add the reserved florets and toss lightly so that you don't break up the whole florets too much. Spoon into 4 warmed pasta bowls, sprinkle over the rest of the Parmesan and serve.

SEARED MEDALLIONS OF SALMON

with hot pepper marmalade and crème fraîche raita

OK, I've stolen the idea for this from another chef, so apologies to Peter Gordon of the Sugar Club in London for basing this on his wonderful signature dish of scallops with chilli jam and crème fraîche. But I've changed it a lot, he said in meek defence, and whatever, it's pretty damn good. Enough said!

Serves 4

sunflower oil for deep frying, plus
   2 tablespoons
1 small bunch of fresh chives
350 g (12 oz) piece skinned salmon fillet,
   taken from a large fish
lemon juice
Maldon salt and freshly ground black pepper

For the hot pepper marmalade:

1 medium red onion, finely chopped
2 cloves garlic, finely chopped
1 teaspoon ground coriander
2 tablespoons olive oil
2 red peppers, seeded and cut into thin strips

2.5 cm (1 inch) piece fresh root ginger,
   peeled and finely grated
1 long, thin red chilli, finely chopped (seeds
   and all)
100 ml (3½ fl oz) red wine vinegar (preferably
   Cabernet Sauvignon)
40 g (1½ oz) soft light brown sugar

For the crème fraîche raita:

4 tablespoons crème fraîche or soured cream
5 cm (2 inch) piece cucumber, peeled, seeded
   and diced
1 small cooked potato, finely diced
Tomatoes Concassées (see page 184),
   use 2 tomatoes
2 tablespoons chopped fresh coriander

For the hot pepper marmalade, sweat the onion, garlic and ground coriander in the oil for about 5 minutes until soft and lightly browned. Add the red peppers, ginger and chilli and cook over a low heat for another 10 minutes until soft. Add the vinegar and the sugar, bring up to a simmer and leave to cook gently for 20 minutes, giving the mixture a stir every now and then.

For the raita, simply mix all the ingredients together, cover and chill in the fridge until needed.

Pour about 1 cm (½ inch) oil into a small pan and heat to 160°C/325°F. Chop the chives into 7.5 cm (3 inch) lengths, then deep-fry them for 15–20 seconds. Drain on kitchen paper. Cut the salmon fillet in half down the natural central seam and then slice each piece across into about 6 thin medallions. Heat a large frying pan until very hot. Add 2 tablespoons oil, then flash-fry the salmon for about 2 minutes on one side only. Quickly lift the slices onto a baking sheet and season with a little lemon juice, salt and pepper.

Spoon some hot pepper marmalade onto each plate, then arrange 3 pieces of the salmon around it. Add a spoonful of the raita, pile the deep-fried chives on top and serve.

FETA FRITTATA

with smoked salmon and herbed crème fraîche

This is really just a nice, big, thick wedge of omelette with lots of tasty bits in it – traditional Italian stuff. The Italians could teach us a thing or two about cooking and eating, and drinking come to think of it, not to mention how to have a good time! You could alternatively cook this in a deep frying pan on top of the stove and brown off the top under the grill, but the finished frittata will not be quite so thick.

Serves 8

1 tablespoon olive oil

1 bunch of spring onions, trimmed and sliced

50 g (2 oz) rocket

8 medium farm-fresh eggs

200 ml (7 fl oz) crème fraîche

2 tablespoons chopped fresh flatleaf parsley

2 Roasted Red Peppers (see page 185), cut into long, thin strips

100 g (4 oz) feta cheese, crumbled

Maldon salt and freshly ground white pepper

1 tablespoon each chopped fresh dill, mint and parsley

275 g (10 oz) Scottish smoked salmon

Preheat the oven to 160°C/325°F/Gas Mark 3. Grease and base-line a 20 cm (8 inch) clip-sided cake tin with non-stick baking parchment, taking the paper over the join and very slightly up the sides just in case your tin is not watertight.

Heat the oil in a pan. Add the spring onions and fry over a high heat for about 2 minutes until soft and lightly tinged with brown. Add the rocket and stir it around in the hot pan until it has only just wilted, then take the pan off the heat.

Break the eggs into a bowl and whisk in 3 tablespoons of the crème fraîche. Stir in the chopped parsley, roasted red peppers, feta cheese and the spring onion and rocket mix. Season well with salt and pepper.

Pour the mixture into the tin and bake in the oven for 40–45 minutes until just set. Remove and leave to cool to room temperature.

Mix the remaining crème fraîche with the chopped herbs and some seasoning to taste. Slice the frittata into 8 slices and place one on each plate. Loosely pile some smoked salmon alongside and serve with a spoonful of the herbed crème fraîche.

PRESSED TERRINE OF POTATO, CHICKEN LIVERS AND PARMA HAM

This was a bit of a culinary triumph – the idea had been floating around in my head since I tasted a potato and *foie gras* terrine at some posh French noshery years ago. This version uses cheap ingredients (except for the Parma ham) and is, I have to say in all modesty, pretty damn good. Ideal for a big dinner-party first course with all the work done in advance, or for a slightly smaller number at lunch time. If you have trouble slicing it, try using an electric knife – they have to be useful for something!

Serves 12

*2 × 225 g (8 oz) firm main crop potatoes,
  such as Romano or Maris Piper*

8 thin slices Parma ham

175 g (6 oz) butter

2 cloves garlic, finely chopped

3 tablespoons chopped fresh flatleaf parsley

Maldon salt and freshly ground white pepper

2 tablespoons sunflower oil

750 g (1½ lb) fresh chicken livers, trimmed

25 g (1 oz) Parmesan, finely grated

To serve:

4 tablespoons Herb Oil (see page 186)

75 g (3 oz) mixed baby salad leaves

You will need to prepare this terrine the day before you want to serve it as it has to be pressed overnight. First thing in the morning, boil the whole, unpeeled potatoes in salted water for 30–40 minutes until tender when pierced with a skewer. Drain them, leave to go cold and then chill them in the fridge for quite a few hours, during which time they will firm up and become much easier to slice. (If you can do this the night before, even better.)

Lightly oil a 7.5 cm (3 inch) deep, 7.5 × 25 cm (3 × 10 inch) terrine dish (a Le Creuset terrine is ideal) and then line it with some clingfilm so that the edges are left overhanging. Now line the dish with the slices of Parma ham, overlapping them slightly and leaving about 7.5 cm (3 inches) overhanging all the way round.

Peel the potatoes and cut each one across into 5 mm (¼ inch) thick slices. Melt the butter with the garlic in a small pan and leave it to cook over a very gentle heat for 10 minutes. Stir in the chopped parsley and plenty of seasoning and set it aside to cool but not set.

Heat half the oil in a large, non-stick frying pan, add half the chicken livers and fry them over a high heat, turning them now and then, for about 2–3 minutes until nicely browned but still rare and juicy in the centre. Season well with salt and pepper and set aside while you cook the rest.

To assemble the terrine, pour a thin layer of the garlic butter into the bottom of the dish and tilt it back and forth until it has completely covered the base. Now layer one-third of the potato slices over the butter and season them well with salt and pepper. Cover the potatoes with half the chicken livers and sprinkle them with half of the Parmesan. Spoon over some more of the garlic butter and repeat these layers once more, remembering to season them as you go. Now cover the top of the terrine with the remaining one-third of the sliced potatoes and then fold the overhanging edges of the Parma ham over the top so that the potatoes are completely covered. Fold over the clingfilm – if there isn't quite enough, cover with another sheet – and then weigh down the terrine. You can do this either by placing a second terrine on top and filling it with heavy objects, or by cutting a piece of cardboard to fit inside the top edge, covering the terrine dish in foil and then weighing it down with metal weights or a few unopened cans. Slide it into the fridge and leave it to chill overnight.

To serve, gently toss the prepared salad leaves with some of the herb oil. Fold the clingfilm back from the top of the terrine and invert it onto a board or serving dish. Using a very sharp knife, carve it into 12 thin slices and place them on the plates. Pile the dressed salad leaves alongside, drizzle around the remaining herb oil and serve, perhaps with some crusty French bread.

SALT AND PEPPER SQUID

with stir-fried vegetables

I'm not quite sure why, but dry-frying salt and pepper together produces a really wonderful aromatic flavour that's more than just salt and pepper. Don't overcrowd the pan when deep-frying or the pieces will stick together, and by the time the rings are golden, the squid will be overcooked and rubbery. Now I know that I don't really have to say this, but I'm going to. Don't use frozen squid – but of course, you wouldn't! It would be quite in order to serve wedges of lemon to squeeze over the squid.

Serves 4

225 g (8 oz) cleaned squid
1½ teaspoons Maldon salt
2 teaspoons Sichuan peppercorns
sunflower oil, for deep frying
2 tablespoons self-raising flour

For the stir-fried vegetables:
50 g (2 oz) mangetout peas

50 g (2 oz) piece red pepper
2 spring onions, chopped
2 tablespoons sunflower oil
1 teaspoon finely chopped root ginger
1 teaspoon finely chopped garlic
50 g (2 oz) fresh beansprouts
2 teaspoons Thai fish sauce
2 teaspoons lime juice
1 tablespoon chopped fresh coriander

Slice the squid across into thin rings and separate the tentacles if large. Heat a dry, heavy-based frying pan over a medium heat. Add the salt and stir it around for a couple of minutes until it begins to look a bit grey. Tip it into a bowl, reheat the pan, then add the Sichuan peppercorns and toss them around until they darken slightly and start to smell aromatic. Grind the salt and peppercorns to a fine powder in a coffee grinder or a pestle and mortar.

Pour some oil into a large pan so that it is about one-third full and heat it to 190°C/375°F. Mix the salt and pepper powder with the flour, place it in a plastic bag and add the squid. Give the bag a good shake so that all the pieces of squid become evenly coated in the highly seasoned flour, and then deep-fry 5–6 pieces at a time in the hot oil for just 30–45 seconds until crisp and golden. Lift out with a slotted spoon onto a paper-lined tray and keep warm in a low oven.

For the stir-fried vegetables, cut the mangetout peas and the piece of red pepper into strips about the same thickness as the beansprouts. Heat a large, deep frying pan or wok until very hot. Add the oil, onion, ginger and garlic and stir around for a few seconds. Then throw in the mangetout and red pepper and stir-fry for 1 minute. Take the pan off the heat and stir in the beansprouts, fish sauce, lime juice and coriander.

Pile the salt and pepper squid slightly to one side of 4 warmed plates, pile a little of the stir-fried vegetables alongside and serve.

Omelettes

The secret of a good omelette is in ingredients with impeccable credentials, and this means farm eggs – not the so-called free-range eggs, but the real hand-gathered ones from the farmyard. Once you've cooked them and seen the difference in the colour (yes, a real yellow omelette), never mind the taste, you'll be converted.

MULL CHEDDAR OMELETTE

with parsley

A simple dish which is a real star. The cheese must be properly matured, unpasteurized Cheddar from a good cheese-maker. Mull Cheddar is probably the best you can get, but there are some other crackers around. Taste this and you'll realize that simple is best.

Serves 1

2 medium farm-fresh eggs
1 tablespoon double cream

Maldon salt and freshly ground white pepper
1 tablespoon oil or melted butter
25 g (1 oz) Mull Cheddar, coarsely grated
1 teaspoon chopped fresh parsley

Break the eggs into a bowl, add the cream and season with a little salt and pepper. Lightly whisk together with a fork until the whites and yolks are only just combined.

Heat a 20 cm (8 inch) frying pan over a low–medium heat. Add the oil or butter and, as soon as it is hot, pour in the eggs and swirl them around a bit so that they coat the bottom of the pan. As soon as they begin to set over the base, start stirring them into the centre of the pan with the back of a fork so that the runny egg can move about and come into contact with the hot base.

As soon as the omelette mixture stops moving about (but is still very moist on top), sprinkle over the grated cheese and the chopped parsley and leave for just a few seconds. Lift the pan off the heat, tilt it towards you at an angle of 45 degrees and, using a fork, release the furthermost edge of the omelette and roll it over towards the lower edge of the pan nearest you. Cover the pan with a plate, then turn the two over together so that omelette is now on the plate, and eat straight away.

CHANTERELLE MUSHROOM OMELETTE

with garlic and chives

Chanterelles have a very distinctive, apricoty flavour and are one of my favourite mushrooms, available from the end of July through to mid October. They are at their best, and cheapest, in September and, being one of the most perfumed of mushrooms, they're great in omelettes. Using other varieties of mushroom will give good results but they won't be in the same league as the chanterelle.

Serves 1

1 tablespoon oil or melted butter
1 small clove garlic, finely chopped
100 g (4 oz) chanterelle mushrooms, wiped
   clean, halved if large

Maldon salt and freshly ground white pepper
2 medium farm-fresh eggs
1 tablespoon double cream
15 g (½ oz) knob of butter
1 small bunch of fresh chives,
   roughly chopped

Melt the oil or melted butter in the frying pan, add the garlic and cook for a few seconds before throwing in the mushrooms. Stir-fry over a high heat for about a minute until just cooked through. Season with salt and pepper.

Break the eggs into a bowl, add the cream and season with a little salt and pepper. Lightly whisk together with a fork until the whites and yolks are only just combined.

Heat a 20 cm (8 inch) frying pan over a low–medium heat. Add the knob of butter and, as soon as it is hot, pour in the eggs and swirl them around a bit so that they coat the bottom of the pan. As soon as they begin to set over the base, start stirring them into the centre of the pan with the back of a fork so that the runny egg can move about and come into contact with the hot base.

As soon as the omelette mixture stops moving about (but is still very moist on top), sprinkle over the mushrooms, garlic and the chopped chives and leave for just a few seconds. Lift the pan off the heat, tilt it towards you at an angle of 45 degrees and, using a fork, release the furthermost edge of the omelette and roll it over towards the lower edge of the pan nearest you. Cover the pan with a plate and then turn the two over together so that omelette is now on the plate, and eat straight away.

SMOKED HADDOCK, PUY LENTIL AND TARRAGON OMELETTE

This variation adds smoky haddock, earthy lentils and aromatic tarragon for a taste sensation. I cooked this omelette in a challenge to find the best omelette in Scotland and was up against chefs who used *foie gras*, truffles and fancy sauces with theirs. Suffice to say that simplicity won the day! Cook a pile of lentils as they keep in the fridge for a couple of days and even freeze well.

Serves 1

2 medium farm-fresh eggs
1 tablespoon double cream
Maldon salt and freshly ground white pepper
1 tablespoon oil or melted butter
50–75 g (2–3 oz) cooked, flaked smoked
    haddock
1 teaspoon chopped fresh tarragon

For the lentils:
225 g (8 oz) Puy lentils
1 halved head of garlic
1 fresh bay leaf
1 sprig of fresh thyme
1 carrot, peeled and roughly chopped

Put the lentils in a pan with 3 times the amount of water, the garlic, bay leaf, thyme, carrot and a pinch of salt. Simmer for 15–20 minutes or until you can crush a lentil between finger and thumb. Take care not to overcook them. Drain, discard the garlic, bay leaf, thyme and carrot and set aside.

Break the eggs into a bowl, add the cream and season with a little salt and pepper. Lightly whisk together with a fork until the whites and yolks are only just combined.

Heat a 20 cm (8 inch) frying pan over a low–medium heat. Add the oil or butter and, as soon as it is hot, pour in the eggs and swirl them around a bit so that they coat the bottom of the pan. As soon as they begin to set over the base, start stirring them into the centre of the pan with the back of a fork so that the runny egg can move about and come into contact with the hot base.

As soon as the omelette mixture stops moving about (but is still very moist on top), sprinkle over the flaked haddock, a couple of tablespoons of the lentils and the chopped tarragon and leave for just a few seconds. Lift the pan off the heat, tilt it towards you at an angle of 45 degrees and, using a fork, release the furthermost edge of the omelette and roll it over towards the lower edge of the pan nearest you. Cover the pan with a plate and then turn the two over together so that omelette is now on the plate, and eat straight away.

THAI CRAB OMELETTE

with spring onions and ginger

You might have guessed by now that I'm well into my Thai flavourings, so I thought I would try them in an omelette, and I was chuffed with the results. Obviously fresh crabmeat is best, but frozen or pasteurized would do here as its flavour has strong support from the spices.

Serves 1

50 ml (2 fl oz) Chicken Stock (see page 181)
¾ teaspoon Thai fish sauce or dark soy sauce
½ teaspoon soft light brown sugar
¼ teaspoon sesame oil
2 medium farm-fresh eggs
Maldon salt and freshly ground white pepper

4 teaspoons sunflower oil
½ teaspoon freshly grated root ginger
25 g (1 oz) mangetout peas, thinly shredded
25 g (1 oz) fresh beansprouts
1 spring onion, halved and cut into
   very fine shreds
50 g (2 oz) fresh white crabmeat
1 tablespoon chopped fresh coriander

Put the chicken stock, ½ teaspoon of the fish sauce or dark soy sauce, a pinch of the sugar and the sesame oil into a small pan, bring up to the boil and simmer very gently for 1 minute. Keep hot over a very low heat.

Break the eggs into a bowl, add the rest of the fish sauce or soy sauce and sugar and some salt and pepper, and beat together until just mixed. Set aside.

Heat 1 teaspoon of the sunflower oil in a small saucepan over a high heat. Add the ginger and mangetout and stir-fry for 1 minute. Remove from the heat and stir in the beansprouts and the spring onion shreds. Bring back to the heat and add the eggs to the pan. Swirl them around a bit so that they coat the bottom of the pan. As soon as they begin to set over the base, start stirring them into the centre of the pan with the back of a fork so that the runny egg can move about and come into contact with the hot base.

As soon as the omelette mixture stops moving about (but is still very moist on top), sprinkle over the crabmeat and the chopped coriander and leave for just a few seconds. Lift the pan off the heat, tilt it towards you at an angle of 45 degrees and, using a fork, release the furthermost edge of the omelette and roll it over towards the lower edge of the pan nearest you. Cover the pan with a plate and then turn the two over together so that omelette is now on the plate. Pour over the sauce and eat straight away.

Scottish Oatcakes

These oatcakes are traditionally cooked on a griddle over an open fire, but you can get a great result by baking them in the oven too. They can be made well in advance, cooled and stored in an airtight container. When made, a nice bit of cheese is all you really need, but use your imagination and the sky is the limit – as the following four recipes demonstrate.

SCOTTISH OATCAKES

with goat's cheese, cherry tomatoes and basil

The lovely, soft, creamy texture of goat's cheese is the perfect foil for the sharp sweetness of cherry tomatoes and basil.

Serves 4

225 g (8 oz) medium oatmeal, plus extra
   for dusting
¼ teaspoon bicarbonate of soda
½ teaspoon salt
15 g (½ oz) bacon fat, lard or butter

150 ml (5 fl oz) water
25 g (1 oz) butter, melted
175 g (6 oz) goat's cheese, crumbled
24 cherry plum tomatoes, halved
1–2 tablespoons extra virgin olive oil
Maldon salt and freshly ground black pepper
8 sprigs of fresh basil

Preheat the oven to 180°C/350°F/Gas Mark 4. Put the oatmeal, bicarbonate of soda and salt into a bowl and mix well. Place the fat, lard or butter and water in a small pan and heat until the fat has melted. Make a well in the centre of the oatmeal, add the liquid and mix together with a palette knife. The mixture will initially seem a bit wet but the oatmeal will gradually absorb all the liquid to give you a soft dough. Divide the mixture into 2 and roll each piece out on a work surface lightly dusted with oatmeal to a 15 cm (6 inch) circle about 5 mm (¼ inch) thick. Don't worry if the edges aren't very neat – they look better that way. Cut into quarters (farls, as they say in Scotland), brush off the excess oatmeal and place on an ungreased baking sheet. Bake for about 20 minutes, turning the oatcakes every 5 minutes or so to stop them from steaming and going stodgy, until crisp and lightly golden. Leave to cool on a wire rack.

To serve, brush the oatcakes with some melted butter and place 2 pieces on each serving plate. Pile the goat's cheese and cherry tomatoes on top, drizzle with a little olive oil and then sprinkle with a little salt and pepper. Garnish with the sprigs of fresh basil.

SCOTTISH OATCAKES

with chicken livers, red onion conserve and rocket

These are a bit messy for finger eating but are good enough for the proper knife and fork treatment. One makes a great starter, two, a smashing lunch, three and you're a pig, but I bet you smile a lot! There will be more red onion conserve than you need, so just spoon the rest into a jar, pour a thin layer of oil on top and store it in the fridge. It will keep for 6–8 weeks and goes really well with all sorts of hot and cold meats, or cheese.

Serves 4

25 g (1 oz) butter
350 g (12 oz) chicken livers, trimmed
Maldon salt and freshly ground black pepper
1 quantity Scottish Oatcakes (see page 60)
25 g (1 oz) rocket leaves
a few drops of olive oil and freshly squeezed
*   lemon juice*

For the red onion conserve
   (makes about 450 g/1 lb):
75 ml (3 fl oz) olive oil
1.5 kg (3 lb) red onions, thinly sliced
120 ml (4 fl oz) sherry vinegar or Cabernet
*   Sauvignon vinegar*
2 tablespoons crème de cassis (optional)

For the red onion conserve, heat the oil in a large, heavy-based pan. Add the onions and cook over a low–medium heat, stirring now and then, for 1 hour until the onions are very soft and richly caramelized. Add the vinegar and simmer for another 10 minutes until the harsh flavour of the vinegar has been boiled off and the conserve has thickened. Stir in the crème de cassis, if using, season to taste with salt and pepper, and keep warm over a low heat.

Heat the butter in a large frying pan, add the chicken livers and fry over a high heat, turning them as they brown, for about 3 minutes until they are nicely browned on the outside but still pink and juicy in the centre. Season with salt and pepper and then arrange over the top of each oatcake. Spoon a little of the warmed onion conserve in among the livers. Toss the rocket leaves with the oil and lemon juice and season to taste with salt and pepper. Pile on top of each oatcake and serve.

SCOTTISH OATCAKES

with blue cheese, walnuts and watercress

There are some cracking Scottish blue cheeses, such as Lanark Blue and Dunsyre Blue, but Bleu de Bresse, Shropshire Blue or Stilton would be just as satisfying.

Serves 4

175 g (6 oz) blue cheese
1 quantity Scottish Oatcakes (see page 60)

50 g (2 oz) walnut pieces
25 g (1 oz) watercress, large stalks removed
a few drops of extra virgin olive oil
Maldon salt and freshly ground black pepper

Break the cheese into small crumbly pieces and divide it between the oatcakes, with the walnut pieces. Toss the watercress leaves with a little oil and a little seasoning. Arrange the oatcakes on a baking tray and slide them under a hot grill for about 1 minute until the cheese just begins to melt. Quickly transfer them to serving plates, pile the watercress on top and serve.

SCOTTISH OATCAKES

with creamy scrambled eggs and smoked salmon

This would also make great breakfast material, again down the knife and fork route. Serve with a compote of fruit and a glass of freshly squeezed orange juice to someone you love.

Serves 4

6 farm-fresh eggs
Maldon salt and freshly ground black pepper
25 g (1 oz) butter

4 tablespoons double cream (optional)
1 quantity Scottish Oatcakes (see page 60)
50–75 g (2–3 oz) thinly sliced Scottish smoked salmon
chopped fresh chives, to garnish

Break the eggs into a bowl, season and beat together lightly with a fork. Melt half the butter in a small non-stick pan. Swirl it around so that it coats the sides a little, add the eggs and cook over a medium heat, stirring all the time, for about 2 minutes or until the eggs are half set. Take off the heat, add the rest of the butter, and the cream if using, and keep stirring, returning the pan to the heat briefly if necessary, until the eggs are soft and creamy. Spoon the scrambled eggs onto each oatcake and loosely pile the smoked salmon on top. Sprinkle with a few chopped chives and serve.

BAKED GOAT'S CHEESE IN FILO PASTRY

with leeks and a tomato and mint sauce *vierge*

I've recently rediscovered filo in my cooking. It was quite a thing in the 1980s and got over-used, but sometimes I find it useful to delve back into the past and take the best bits of old dishes and rework them. Here you need good, ripe goat's cheese – there are now some cracking Scottish, Irish and English ones around – and thin, firm leeks. You can make up the parcels in advance and finish cooking them just before serving. The mint in the sauce works just a treat!

Serves 4

75 g (3 oz) butter
225 g (8 oz) leeks, cleaned and sliced
4 tablespoons double cream or crème fraîche
Maldon salt and freshly ground black pepper
6 sheets of filo pastry
4 × 40 g (1½ oz) slices goat's cheese or
   2 × 100 g (4 oz) goat's cheeses, halved
   into 2 smaller discs

For the tomato and mint sauce *vierge*:

75 ml (3 fl oz) olive oil
1 tablespoon white wine vinegar
Tomato Concassée (see page 184), use
   1 tomato
½ small red onion, very finely chopped
¼ teaspoon Maldon salt and some freshly
   ground black pepper
1 tablespoon chopped fresh mint

Melt 25 g (1 oz) of the butter in a pan, add the leeks and cook over a medium heat for about 3 minutes until they are just soft. Take the pan off the heat and stir in the cream or crème fraîche and plenty of seasoning. Cool slightly. Preheat the oven to 220°C/425°F/Gas Mark 7.

Meanwhile, melt the remaining butter. Lay one sheet of filo pastry on a work surface and brush with some of the melted butter. Cover with another sheet of pastry, brush with more butter and then cover with a third sheet. Set aside and repeat with the rest of the pastry. Now cut two 20 cm (8 inch) discs from each stack of pastry and place one piece of cheese in the centre of each one. Spoon a quarter of the leeks on top of each piece of cheese and then, working around the edge of the pastry, pleat and fold it neatly over the top, sealing as you go with a little water. Brush each parcel all over with more butter and place on a lightly buttered baking sheet. Bake in the oven for 10–12 minutes until crisp and golden.

For the sauce *vierge*, put the oil, vinegar, tomatoes, red onion, salt and pepper into a small pan and allow them just to warm through over a very gentle heat. Stir in the mint. Place a filo parcel in the centre of each plate and spoon some of the sauce around each parcel.

POTATO SCONES

topped with steam-fried eggs

Basic but brilliant. Use farm-fresh eggs and serve with maybe a rasher or two of bacon on the side. The fried-egg trick is stolen from the rather clever Paul Rankin and has revolutionized fried-egg-making for me. The 'long-haired' one also has one of Britain's best restaurants, Roscoff's in Belfast, which serves mighty fine scoff.

Serves 4

100 g (4 oz) butter
8 farm-fresh eggs
4 teaspoons water

For the potato scones:

225 g (8 oz) floury main crop potatoes
50 g (2 oz) butter
Maldon salt and freshly ground black pepper
50 g (2 oz) plain flour

For the scones, peel the potatoes, cut them into chunks and cook them in boiling salted water for 20 minutes or until tender. Drain them well, return them to the pan and then toss them around over the heat for a few minutes to drive off all the excess moisture. Now either pass them through a potato ricer, or mash and then press through a sieve into a bowl. Beat in the butter and a pinch of salt and then work in the flour to make a soft dough. Turn the mixture out onto a lightly floured board, divide into 2 and knead once or twice until smooth. Roll out each piece into a circle about 5 mm (¼ inch) thick and then cut each circle into quarters. Prick well with a fork.

Heat a cast-iron griddle over a medium–high heat and lightly grease with a little butter. Lift on 4 of the scones and cook for 3 minutes on each side until golden brown and firm. Wrap in a tea towel to keep them warm while you cook the rest.

For the eggs, melt half the butter in a large frying pan with a tight-fitting lid. Break in 4 of the eggs, trying to make sure they don't touch, and leave them until the whites have set. Then add 2 teaspoons of the water, put on the lid and leave for 45 seconds to 1 minute, during which time the water will turn to steam and lightly cook the tops of the eggs. Lift out, keep warm and repeat with the rest of the eggs.

Place a couple of the scones on each plate and spread with a little extra butter if you wish. Lift an egg onto each, season with some salt and freshly ground black pepper and serve.

Vast areas of Scotland's staggeringly

beautiful countryside are not only

unpolluted, but unpopulated,

allowing a proliferation of furred

and feathered game, which provides

meat of an unrivalled quality.

MAIN COURSES

FISH

POACHED SEA TROUT
with herb mayonnaise, onion 'grass' and gaufrette potatoes

Sea trout has a more delicate flavour than salmon and, as far as I know, nobody has managed to farm it yet, so it's bound to be wild. That is why I've chosen to poach it – not a cooking technique I use a lot – but, if done carefully, you get lovely moist fish with all its flavour intact. And what better to go with poached fish than a mayonnaise flavoured with herbs? The onion 'grass' is very easy and adds texture, as do the gaufrette potatoes which are just posh crisps really.

Serves 6

3 × 750 g (1½ lb) sea trout
sunflower oil for deep frying
4 × fist-sized firm potatoes, such as Golden
   Wonder or Maris Piper, peeled
1 medium onion
25 g (1 oz) plain flour
Maldon salt and freshly ground white pepper

For the court bouillon:
1.75 litres (3 pints) water
½ lemon, sliced
1 fresh bay leaf

20 peppercorns
a handful of fresh parsley and tarragon stalks

For the herb mayonnaise:
1 medium farm-fresh egg yolk
1 teaspoon Dijon mustard
225 ml (8 fl oz) Herb Oil (see page 186)

For the salad garnish:
100 g (4 oz) mixed baby salad leaves,
   such as lamb's lettuce, rocket, cos and
   fennel herb
a few drops of olive oil
a few drops of lemon juice

Fillet the sea trout, taking care to use short, gentle strokes because the flesh is quite soft, then skin them. Lay each fillet skinned-side up and, starting at the wider head end, roll each one up into a coil and secure it at the tail end by pushing a cocktail stick right through into the centre. Stand each one upright so that it looks like a tower with a rose-shaped top and set to one side.

   Put all the ingredients for the court bouillon in a small roasting tin, bring up to a rapid simmer and keep hot over a low heat.

For the herb mayonnaise, mix the egg yolk and mustard together in a bowl and then very gradually whisk in the herb oil until the finished mixture is thick and silky smooth. Cover with some clingfilm and chill until needed.

Pour some of the sunflower oil into a large pan and heat to 180°C/350°F. Meanwhile, cut each potato across into 2 shorter halves and then thinly slice on a mandolin fitted with a ridged blade. With every slice, give the potato a 90-degree turn so that the slices take on a lattice design. Dry them well on kitchen paper and deep-fry a handful at a time until crisp and golden. Lift out with a slotted spoon onto a paper-lined tray and keep warm in a low oven. To make the onion 'grass', cut the onion in half and thinly slice on the mandolin. Separate the strands into a bowl, add the flour and some salt and pepper and work everything together with your fingertips so that all the pieces get well coated in the flour. Deep-fry a handful at a time until crisp and golden and keep warm alongside the potatoes.

Bring the court bouillon back up to a simmer, add the sea trout rolls still in an upright position and poach them for just 6 minutes. While they are cooking, toss the salad leaves with a little oil, lemon juice and some seasoning until they glisten like wet skin.

Lift the sea trout out of the tin, let the excess liquid drain away and then set slightly to one side of each serving plate. Pile the onion 'grass' on top of each piece of salmon, pile some of the potatoes and salad alongside and garnish with 2 small quenelles of the herb mayonnaise.

ROAST MONKFISH

with cumin-roasted carrots and a spicy carrot juice sauce

Sauces made with vegetable juices are all the rage at the moment and deservedly so. Store-bought carrot juice is fine (you'll find it in health food shops) but if you have a juicer try out beetroot, asparagus, red pepper and celery too. In this dish the sauce is finished with butter but you could use olive oil instead, which doesn't emulsify like the butter but gives the finished sauce a nice speckled effect.

Serves 4

750 g (1½ lb) large monkfish fillets

Maldon salt and freshly ground white pepper

sunflower oil

16 sprigs of fresh coriander

For the cumin-roasted carrots:

450 g (1 lb) medium-sized carrots, peeled

1 tablespoon sunflower oil

2 teaspoons ground cumin

For the spicy carrot juice sauce:

1 teaspoon yellow mustard seeds

1 teaspoon cumin seeds

1 teaspoon coriander seeds

2 teaspoons sunflower oil

1 cm (½ inch) piece fresh root ginger, peeled
  and chopped

300 ml (10 fl oz) fresh carrot juice
  (home-made or bought)

300 ml (10 fl oz) Chicken Stock
  (see page 181)

50 g (2 oz) unsalted butter

1 tablespoon chopped fresh coriander

For the sauce, heat a dry, heavy-based pan over a high heat. Add the yellow mustard seeds and fry for a few seconds until they begin to pop. Tip them into a small bowl and set aside. Add the cumin and coriander seeds to the dry pan and fry until they have darkened very slightly and are starting to smell aromatic. Tip them into a second bowl and set aside. Heat the oil in a medium-sized pan. Add the ginger and fry for a couple of minutes until lightly golden. Add the roasted cumin and coriander seeds and fry for another minute. Add the carrot juice and stock, bring to the boil and boil rapidly until reduced by about three-quarters. Remove from the heat and set aside.

For the cumin-roasted carrots, preheat the oven to 220°C/425°F/Gas Mark 7. Cut each carrot in half into 2 shorter pieces and then cut each piece in half lengthways. Drop into a pan of boiling salted water and cook for 2–3 minutes. Drain and refresh under running cold water. Dry well on kitchen paper. Transfer the carrots to a small roasting tin and add the oil, the ground cumin and some salt and pepper. Toss together so the carrots get evenly coated in the spices and then slide the tin into the oven for 20–30 minutes or until the carrots are cooked to your liking. I like them with a little hint of crunch inside.

Meanwhile, cut the monkfish into twelve 2 cm (¾ inch) slices and flatten slightly with the palm of your hand into discs. Heat a heavy-based frying pan over a high heat. Season the monkfish with some salt and pepper. As soon as the pan is hot, brush it with a little oil, add 2 or 3 pieces of monkfish and cook them for 2 minutes on the first side, then 1 minute on the second side, until just cooked through. Lift them onto a plate, cover with some foil and repeat with the rest of the slices. Leave to relax somewhere warm for a few minutes.

Strain the carrot juice sauce through a fine sieve into a clean pan and bring it back to the boil. Lower the heat and then whisk in the butter, a little piece at a time, to make a smooth, glossy sauce. Stir in the roasted yellow mustard seeds and chopped fresh coriander and season to taste with a little salt and pepper.

Place a few of the carrots in the centre of each plate and place a sprig of coriander and a slice of the monkfish on top. Stack more carrots, coriander sprigs and monkfish until you have used 3 slices of fish per person, finishing with the carrots. Pour some of the sauce around the edge of the plate, garnish with the remaining sprigs of fresh coriander and serve.

SPICY SALMON

with a chilled cucumber salad

This dish started out as a Cajun Salmon but I changed the original spices after mixing up this recipe with another during a cookery show. And I'm very glad it happened too, because this is better than the original. The salmon is pretty spicy and I like some chilli in the cucumber salad as well. However, if you are not a big chilli fan, leave it out of the salad but not the salmon.

Serves 6

6 x 175 g (6 oz) pieces thick salmon fillet, unskinned
1 tablespoon paprika powder
1 teaspoon dried chilli flakes
½ teaspoon dried thyme
½ teaspoon dried oregano
1 teaspoon black peppercorns
½ teaspoon cumin seeds

2 teaspoons Maldon salt, plus extra for sprinkling
3 tablespoons olive oil, plus extra to serve

For the chilled cucumber salad:
2 cucumbers
1 large clove garlic, very finely chopped
1 tablespoon lemon or lime juice
1 long, thin red chilli, seeded and finely chopped
2 tablespoons chopped fresh coriander

Score the skin of the salmon and set to one side. Put the paprika, chilli flakes, thyme, oregano, black peppercorns, cumin seeds and 2 teaspoons of salt into a mortar or coffee grinder and grind to a fine powder. Sprinkle over the base of a large plate. Brush the skin of the salmon with some of the olive oil and then dip only the skin side into the salt and spices, making sure that each piece gets coated in an even layer.

For the chilled cucumber salad, peel the cucumbers, cut them in half and scoop out the seeds with a melon-baller or a teaspoon. Cut them lengthways into long, thin shreds by hand, by using a Japanese vegetable turner or on the widest grating attachment of a mandolin and then dry well in a clean tea towel. Set aside in the fridge to chill until needed.

Heat a smooth, cast-iron griddle on the barbecue or on a hob until hot. Add a little olive oil and then the salmon, skin-side down. Cook over a medium heat for about 5 minutes until the skin is nice and crisp. Brush the flesh of the salmon pieces with the remaining oil, turn the fish over and cook for another 2–3 minutes, until just cooked through. Lift it onto a baking sheet straight away so that it doesn't continue to cook.

Add the garlic, lemon or lime juice, chilli, coriander and a pinch of salt to the cucumber and toss together well. Pile the salad in the centre of each plate and place a piece of salmon on top. Drizzle around a little more olive oil and serve.

BAKED HAKE

with spinach, spaghetti of carrots and shellfish cream

When I cooked this dish for the army boys on Benbecula, I was out to impress, so I used lots of different shellfish in the sauce. Very tasty and very cheffy. I would suggest that you stick to just one type – mussels would be my choice and you'll need about 1.5 kg (3 lb). The spaghetti of carrots can be cooked in advance and reheated, as can the sauce, but this is still a dish that requires quite a bit of culinary juggling. Hake is a personal favourite of mine, but a bit scarce. Cod works as an alternative.

Serves 6

50 g (2 oz) butter
6 × 175 g (6 oz) hake fillets, skinned
juice of ½ lemon
Maldon salt and freshly ground black pepper
450 ml (15 fl oz) dry white wine
2 tablespoons olive oil
1 clove garlic, crushed
900 g (2 lb) fresh spinach, washed and any large stalks removed
a small knob of butter

For the spaghetti of carrots:
175 g (6 oz) carrots, peeled
25 g (1 oz) butter
1 tablespoon lemon juice

For the shellfish cream sauce:
450 g (1 lb) fresh mussels
450 g (1 lb) razor clams
450 g (1 lb) cockles
175 g (6 oz) shelled scallops, cleaned
300 ml (10 fl oz) double cream
2–3 tablespoons chopped fresh chervil
a few drops of lemon juice

Heavily grease a shallow baking dish with some of the butter and place the hake fillets on top. Sprinkle them with the lemon juice, dot generously with the rest of the butter and season with some salt and pepper. Pour over 6 tablespoons of the wine and set aside. Preheat the oven to 230°C/450°F/Gas Mark 8.

Prepare the carrots by grating them into long, thin, spaghetti-like strands on a mandolin. If you don't have a mandolin, simply cut the carrots lengthways into thin slices and then cut each slice lengthways into very thin strands.

For the sauce, scrub all the shellfish and wash in plenty of cold water. Discard any that don't stay closed when given a sharp tap. Place the shellfish, one sort at a time, into a large pan with a splash more of the wine, cover and cook over a high heat. Allow 3–4 minutes for the mussels and razor clams and about 2 minutes for the cockles. Discard any shellfish that remain closed. Pour the cooking liquor left in the pan into a clean pan, leaving behind the last couple of tablespoons, which might contain some sand. Bring back to the boil, add the scallops, cover and poach them for 2–3 minutes until firm and just cooked. Lift the scallops onto a plate and pour the cooking liquor into a jug. When the shellfish are cool enough to handle, remove them from their shells and cut the scallops and razor clams into small, neat pieces.

Place 450 ml (15 fl oz) of the shellfish cooking liquor in a pan with the rest of the white wine and bring up to the boil. Leave to boil vigorously until reduced to about 6 tablespoons. Add the double cream, bring it back to the boil and leave to boil until it has reduced and thickened to coat the back of a wooden spoon. Keep the sauce warm over a very low heat.

Slide the hake into the oven and bake it for 5–6 minutes until opaque and firm in the centre. Meanwhile, melt the 'spaghetti' butter in a pan, add the carrots, the lemon juice and some seasoning and cook over a medium heat, stirring until the carrots are just soft and covered in a rich, buttery glaze – about 10 minutes. Keep them warm.

Heat the olive oil in another large pan, add the garlic and the spinach and cook, stirring, until the spinach has wilted. Tip it into a colander, press out the excess liquid, then transfer it to a chopping board and roughly chop it. Return it to the pan with a small knob of butter and some salt and pepper and toss together over a low heat for a few seconds. Stir the cooked shellfish into the cream sauce and allow it to warm through.

To serve, spoon the spinach into the centres of 4 warmed plates. Place a piece of fish on top of the spinach and then twist some of the carrots into a pile on top of each one using a fork. Stir the chopped chervil into the sauce, taste it for seasoning, add a few drops of lemon juice and spoon some around the edges of the plates.

ROAST MONKFISH

with *salsa verde* chickpeas and deep-fried Parma ham

Chickpeas are tricky little beggars to cook – the older they are, the longer they take – but I would always advise erring on the side of overcooking as there are few things worse than undercooked chickpeas. The problem is easily solved by using precooked tinned ones, not quite as tasty but much less of a fuss. When processing the *salsa verde*, be careful not to overwork it. You want a nice, chunky texture, not baby food. The *salsa verde* chickpeas and Parma ham can all be prepared in advance, leaving just the cooking of the monkfish to the last minute.

Serves 4

900 g (2 lb) monkfish fillets
sunflower oil for frying
4 thin slices Parma ham
a little Herb Oil (see page 186), to serve

For the *salsa verde* chickpeas:
450 g (1 lb) dried chickpeas, soaked
   overnight
3–4 cloves garlic, peeled but left whole
4 small, fresh bay leaves

25 g (1 oz) fresh flatleaf parsley
15 g (½ oz) fresh basil leaves
15 g (½ oz) fresh mint leaves
2 cloves garlic, crushed
2 tablespoons salted capers, washed
1 × 50 g (2 oz) can anchovy fillets, drained
1 tablespoon red wine vinegar
3–4 tablespoons extra virgin olive oil
1 teaspoon Dijon mustard
Maldon salt and freshly ground black pepper

First prepare the chickpeas. Drain and place them in a pan with enough cold water to cover. Bring to the boil and cook vigorously for 10 minutes. Drain and rinse under cold water. Return them to the pan and cover with more water (boiling from the kettle will speed things up a little bit). Bring them back to the boil, add the whole garlic cloves and the bay leaves and leave to simmer until tender. This can be anywhere from 1½ to 3 hours, depending on how old the chickpeas are.

Meanwhile, for the *salsa verde*, remove any large stalks from the parsley, basil and mint and place the leaves in a food processor with the crushed garlic, capers and anchovies. Blend everything together for a few seconds until smooth, then scrape the mixture into a bowl and gradually whisk in the vinegar and the oil. Stir in the mustard and season to taste with a little salt and some freshly ground pepper. Set aside.

Trim any membrane off the outside of the monkfish fillets and then cut them across into neat 100 g (4 oz) chunks.

When the chickpeas are just about ready, pour 2 cm (¾ inch) sunflower oil into a medium-sized pan and heat it to 180°C/350°F. Deep-fry the Parma ham, 2 slices at a time, for about

30 seconds, until nice and crisp. Drain on kitchen paper and set aside. Now heat a large, heavy-based frying pan until it is very hot. Add some oil and the monkfish pieces – don't overcrowd the pan (if your pan is not very large, do this in 2 batches). Fry over a high heat for about 4 minutes on each side until the pieces are nicely browned but only just cooked through in the centre.

Drain the chickpeas well and discard the garlic cloves and the bay leaves. Return the chickpeas to the pan with the *salsa verde* and stir together over a low heat until they have just heated through; don't leave them over the heat for too long or the sauce will lose its lovely bright green colour. Spoon the chickpeas into the centre of 4 warmed plates, arrange the pieces of monkfish on top and garnish with the Parma ham. Drizzle a little herb oil around the mound on each plate and serve.

BAKED WHOLE TURBOT
with melted butter and new potatoes

While filming on a Barra trawler, one of the young fishermen, Ali McNeil, baked a turbot for me in the tiny ship's galley. He simply bunged it into a roasting tin and banged it in the oven for 40 minutes. No seasoning, butter, herbs or lemon juice. I was expecting it to be dry and tasteless. He served me up a piece with potatoes and butter and it was a revelation – it was *so* tasty! It really hit home that when you've got top-quality ingredients you don't need to do anything fancy. In the recipe I've added butter, seasoning and lemon juice – just to get a bit more sauce – but the one thing you do need is a super-fresh turbot!

Serves 4

50 g (2 oz) butter
1 x 1.5 kg (3 lb) turbot, cleaned and gutted

juice of ½ lemon
Maldon salt and freshly ground white pepper
450 g (1 lb) new potatoes, scrubbed

Preheat the oven to 180°C/350°F/Gas Mark 4. Take a large roasting tin which is big enough to accommodate the turbot and grease it generously with some of the butter. Cut the head off the fish, lay the turbot in the tin and then dot the top of it with the rest of the butter. Pour over the lemon juice and season the fish with some salt and pepper. Slide the tray into the oven and leave it to roast, uncovered, for 30 minutes. Meanwhile, cook the potatoes in some boiling salted water for 20 minutes or until tender.

Remove the turbot from the oven, run a knife down its backbone and transfer the top 2 fillets to serving plates. Lift off the bone and then put the remaining 2 fillets on the other 2 plates. Serve with the boiled new potatoes and the cooking juices poured over.

ROAST SALMON

with lobster vinaigrette and courgette fritters

Lobster vinaigrette may seem a bit extravagant – and, well, in a way it is – but it makes one lobster go round four people and the flavour that it gives to the sauce is heaven.

The courgette fritters can be made a few hours ahead and reheated in the oven, leaving you with the frying of the salmon and the assembly of the vinaigrette just prior to serving those lucky guests of yours.

Serves 4

sunflower oil
4 × 150 g (5 oz) pieces salmon fillet
lemon juice
Maldon salt and freshly ground white pepper

For the lobster vinaigrette:
1 × 550 g (1 ¼ lb) cooked lobster
120 ml (4 fl oz) olive oil
1 Roasted Red Pepper (see page 185), diced
Tomatoes Concassées (see page 184),
use 3 tomatoes

1 tablespoon chopped fresh coriander
1 tablespoon chopped fresh basil
2 tablespoons balsamic vinegar

For the courgette fritters:
3 medium courgettes, coarsely grated
1 teaspoon Maldon salt, plus a good pinch for
the egg whites
2 medium farm-fresh eggs, separated
150 ml (5 fl oz) double cream
75 g (3 oz) plain flour
2 spring onions, finely chopped
sunflower oil for shallow frying

For the lobster vinaigrette, remove the meat from the lobster claws and tail and cut it into 5 mm (¼ inch) dice. Set aside until you are ready to serve. Preheat the oven to 110°C/225°F/ Gas Mark ¼.

For the courgette fritters, mix the grated courgettes with the teaspoon of salt and leave to drain in a sieve for 15 minutes. Rinse off the salt, squeeze out the excess water and dry well on kitchen paper. Whisk the egg yolks and cream together in a bowl and then whisk in the flour to make a smooth batter. Stir in the spring onions and the courgettes. Whisk the egg whites and the rest of the salt together in a separate bowl until they form soft peaks – make sure they don't get too stiff or they won't blend in with the rest of the mixture. Fold 1 large tablespoon of whites into the courgette mixture to loosen it slightly and then gently fold in the remainder. Pour about 1 cm (½ inch) of sunflower oil into a large frying pan. Using half the mixture, drop in 2 large spoonfuls of the batter, spacing them a little apart, and fry for 3–4 minutes on each side over a medium heat until golden. Drain on kitchen paper and keep warm in the oven while you cook the other 2 and then cook the salmon.

Heat a frying pan until it is very hot. Add a splash of oil and the salmon and sear for 3 minutes on each side. Lift onto a baking tray and season with a little lemon juice, salt and pepper.

To finish the dish, put the olive oil for the vinaigrette into a small pan with the diced red pepper and leave over a very low heat for a couple of minutes to allow the flavour to infuse the oil. Add the lobster and the tomatoes and warm through. Stir in the coriander, basil, balsamic vinegar and some seasoning. Place a courgette fritter in the centre of each warmed plate and rest a piece of the salmon on top. Spoon a little of the lobster vinaigrette around the edge of the plate and serve.

GRIDDLED TROUT

with herb *beurre blanc*

The real secret of this lies in spanking-fresh, native brown trout. In the TV series I managed to cook one that had been caught only 20 minutes earlier, and it was – well, you can guess! For maximum flavour, trout should be less than 24 hours out of the water, making them firm, glossy and flavoursome. This is the perfect dish for a river or loch-side barbie. The butter sauce is easy, once you've got the knack, and goes with all kinds of fish. Then you can experiment with different herbs, spices, pastes and purées for flavouring it.

Serves 4

Maldon salt and freshly ground white pepper
4 brown trout (or rainbow trout), cleaned
  and trimmed
olive oil
juice of ½ lemon

For the herb *beurre blanc*:
2 shallots, very finely chopped
3 tablespoons dry white wine
3 tablespoons white wine vinegar
6 white peppercorns, lightly crushed
175 g (6 oz) chilled unsalted butter, diced
2 tablespoons chopped fresh tarragon

For the *beurre blanc*, put the shallots, white wine, vinegar and peppercorns into a small pan and boil rapidly until reduced to about 2 tablespoons of liquid. Reduce the heat to low and whisk in the butter, a few pieces at a time, to give a smooth, velvety sauce. Season with salt and pepper, pass through a fine sieve into another pan and keep warm in a bowl of warm water while you cook the fish.

Heat a ridged, cast-iron griddle until very hot. Season the trout inside and out. Drizzle a little olive oil over the griddle, add the fish and cook for 4 minutes on each side.

Season the fish once more and squeeze over a little lemon juice. Transfer to warmed plates. Add the chopped tarragon to the sauce and spoon some over the trout, putting the rest to one side of the fish.

SEARED FILLET OF TURBOT

on a bed of braised peas, lettuce and bacon

I'm particularly fond of this combination of salty bacon, sweet peas and lettuce and fried fish. You can use cos or romaine lettuce instead of little gem, or even iceberg at a push. If fresh peas aren't available, then frozen petit pois make a good substitute, but reduce the chicken stock for 3 minutes before adding them and then cook them for just 3 minutes before adding the lettuce. The garnish also works well with other firm-fleshed fish, such as halibut, monkfish, John Dory or brill.

Serves 4

1 tablespoon sunflower oil
1 tablespoon Clarified Butter (see page 183)
4 × 175 g (6 oz) fillets of turbot
lemon juice
Maldon salt and freshly ground white pepper

For the braised peas, lettuce and bacon:
1 tablespoon extra virgin olive oil
50 g (2 oz) rindless streaky bacon or
　pancetta, chopped

25 g (1 oz) butter
½ onion, very finely chopped
1 small clove garlic, crushed
350 g (12 oz) shelled fresh peas or frozen
　petit pois
a pinch of caster sugar
6 tablespoons Chicken Stock (see page 181)
　or water
2 little gem lettuce hearts, finely shredded
2 tablespoons chopped fresh chives

For the braised peas, heat the olive oil in a pan, add the bacon and fry until crisp and lightly golden. Add the butter and the onion and cook for another 2–3 minutes until the onion has softened and is very lightly browned. Add the garlic, peas, sugar, stock or water and some seasoning, cover and cook over a gentle heat for 6 minutes if using fresh peas and about 3 minutes if using frozen, until they are tender.

Heat the sunflower oil in large frying pan. Add the clarified butter and the turbot fillets and fry over a high heat for 3–4 minutes on each side until just cooked through. Lift them out of the pan onto a plate to prevent them from cooking any further, season with a little lemon juice, salt and pepper and keep warm.

Stir the shredded lettuce and chives into the peas and cook for 1 more minute. Check the peas for seasoning and then spoon the mixture into the centres of 4 warmed plates. Place the turbot fillets on top and serve.

STEAMED FLOUNDER

with spring onions, ginger and chilli

Now here's something else that I'd never cooked before, so I looked it up in my fish books, which were all unanimous in pronouncing the poor old flounder a second-rate fish. Well, I have to take them to task because with the addition of all these zingy Chinese flavours it is really rather good. To serve four simply double up the pans and ingredients.

Serves 2

2.5 cm (1 inch) piece fresh root ginger, peeled

3 spring onions, trimmed

½–1 long, thin red chilli

1 clove garlic

1 lime

2 tablespoons good-quality light soy sauce

2 teaspoons sesame oil

2 tablespoons olive oil, plus extra for the
   noodles

15 g (½ oz) chopped fresh chives, plus extra
   to garnish

freshly ground white pepper

1 × 750 g (1½ lb) flounder, filleted or left whole

100 g (4 oz) medium, dried egg noodles

Bring 2 pots of water to the boil. Make sure one of them is the right size to support either a plate or a bamboo steamer.

Cut the piece of ginger into fine julienne strips, thinly slice the spring onions on the diagonal, thinly slice the chilli, chop the garlic and squeeze the juice from half of the lime. Cut the other piece of lime in half once more and set aside.

The easiest way to prepare the fish for steaming is to place a large sheet of clingfilm over the plate or into the base of the steamer, so that the edges are left overhanging. Place half of the following flavourings and oils: ginger, spring onions, chilli, garlic, lime juice, soy sauce, sesame and olive oils in the centre of the clingfilm and add a large pinch of chopped chives and some white pepper. Lay the fish (or fish fillets) on top. Sprinkle over the remainder of the flavourings and the oils and then gather in the edges of the clingfilm and twist them together over the top of the fish to make a watertight packet where none of the juices can leak out. Rest the fish on top of one of the pans of water, cover and cook for 8–10 minutes.

After the fish has been cooking for 4 minutes, drop the noodles into the second pan of water, add a few drops of olive oil, bring back to the boil, cover and set aside off the heat for 4 minutes. Drain the noodles well and return them to the pan.

Lift the fish off the steamer with a fish slice or slotted spoon, hold it over the pan of noodles and carefully undo the clingfilm parcel. Allow all the cooking juices to drip into the noodles. Set down the fish and toss the noodles with the juices. Swirl them into the centre of a large serving plate (for a whole fish) or 2 serving plates (for fillets) and place the fish on top. Season lightly, sprinkle with the rest of the chopped chives and serve with the remaining pieces of lime for squeezing.

STEAMED COD ON A BED OF WILTED SPINACH

with a tomato and blood orange dressing

This dish was developed as part of a healthy eating demonstration which I gave in Glasgow. The fact that the attendance topped the 850 mark reinforced in my mind just how conscious people are these days of eating healthily. Well, you can rest easy with this dish – provided it's served with some plain boiled new potatoes (add a couple of tablespoons of chopped basil for extra flavour), it meets all Glasgow University's criteria for a perfectly balanced meal. And oh, it tastes not bad either. For cooking the cod, you can use a purpose-made steamer consisting of two pans stacked one on top of the other, a bamboo steamer resting over a large saucepan or frying pan, or a plate resting on an upturned bowl placed into the bottom of a larger saucepan. Whichever you choose must be covered with a well-fitting lid so that the fish cooks in hot steam.

Serves 4

4 × 175 g (6 oz) pieces thick cod fillet,
   unskinned
2 tablespoons olive oil
2–3 cloves garlic, crushed
450 g (1 lb) fresh spinach, washed and any
   large stalks removed

2 tablespoons freshly squeezed lemon juice
Maldon salt and freshly ground black pepper

For the tomato and blood orange dressing:
225 g (8 oz) cherry tomatoes
2 tablespoons blood orange juice
1 tablespoon extra virgin olive oil

For the dressing, put the cherry tomatoes, blood orange juice and olive oil into a liquidizer and blitz everything for a few seconds until the tomatoes have just broken up. Press back into a small pan through a chinois or very fine sieve to get rid of all the skin and the little seeds, and season to taste. Set to one side while you cook the fish and the spinach.

Pour some water into your steamer and bring it to the boil. Add the fish, skin-side up, cover with a tight-fitting lid and steam for 7–8 minutes until just firm and opaque. Meanwhile, heat the oil in a large pan, add the garlic and fry for about 1 minute. Add the prepared spinach and stir-fry over a high heat until it has wilted down into the bottom of the pan. Tip it into a colander and press out the excess water. Return it to the pan with half the lemon juice and some seasoning and stir over a medium heat until it has just heated through. At the same time, place the pan of blood orange dressing over a low heat and allow it to warm through to blood temperature, but do not allow it to boil.

To serve, spoon the spinach into the centres of 4 warmed plates. Lift the cod out of the steamer and peel the skin off each piece. Season with the remaining lemon juice and salt and pepper, and place on top of the spinach. Pour some of the dressing over and around the fish.

POTATO AND MACKEREL CURRY

with cardamom rice

This may seem a bit complicated for a curry, where you would normally fling everything into the pot and let it bubble away. However, by cooking the fish, potatoes and sauce separately and then bringing them together at the end, you avoid having a pot of fish and potato glue at the end. If you want to make this in advance, keep all the ingredients separate until ready to serve, then reheat together while the rice is cooking.

Serves 4

450 g (1 lb) waxy main crop potatoes, such as Romano

2 whole cloves

1 teaspoon each of fennel, cumin and coriander seeds

a very small piece cinnamon stick

½ teaspoon ground turmeric

2 × 350–450 g (12 oz–1 lb) mackerel, filleted

15 g (½ oz) plain flour, seasoned with ¼ teaspoon Maldon salt and freshly ground black pepper

5 tablespoons groundnut or sunflower oil

350 g (12 oz) onions (about 2 medium), chopped

2.5 cm (1 inch) piece fresh root ginger, peeled and finely grated

2–3 green chillies, seeded and finely chopped

¾ teaspoon Maldon salt

175 g (6 oz) Greek natural yoghurt

300 ml (10 fl oz) Fish Stock (see page 180)

3 tablespoons chopped fresh coriander

For the cardamom rice:

225 g (8 oz) basmati rice

15 g (½ oz) butter

6 green cardamom pods, cracked

½ teaspoon Maldon salt

350 ml (12 fl oz) boiling water

Boil the unpeeled potatoes until they are tender when pierced with a skewer (about 25 minutes). Meanwhile, heat a dry, heavy-based frying pan until it is very hot. Add the cloves, fennel, cumin and coriander seeds and cinnamon stick and dry-roast for a minute or two until they darken slightly and start to smell aromatic. Tip them into a coffee grinder or mortar and grind to a fine powder. Stir in the turmeric powder. Drain the potatoes and leave to cool, then peel them and cut into 2 cm (¾ inch) chunks. Set aside.

Coat the mackerel fillets in the seasoned flour. Heat about 3–4 tablespoons of the oil in a large, deep frying pan or shallow casserole dish, add the fillets and fry for a couple of minutes on each side until golden brown. Carefully lift out onto a plate and set aside.

Add the potatoes to the pan and cook over a medium heat until they are nicely golden on all sides. Lift out and set aside. Add the rest of the oil to the pan and add the onions, ginger and green chillies and fry for 5–6 minutes until the onions are soft and lightly browned.

Meanwhile, put the rice into a sieve and rinse under cold water until the water runs clear. Tip into a bowl, cover with cold water and leave to soak for 5 minutes. Heat the butter in a pan, add the cardamom pods and fry for 1 minute. Drain the rice, add to the pan and stir gently until all the grains are coated in the butter. Add ½ teaspoon salt and the boiling water. Bring up to the boil, cover and cook over a low heat for 12 minutes. Remove from the heat and leave to stand until the curry is ready.

Break the mackerel fillets into chunky pieces. Add the prepared spices and ¼ teaspoon salt to the onions and cook for 1 minute. Now add the yoghurt, 1 large spoonful at a time, frying it for a minute or two between each addition. Stir in the fish stock and then return the potatoes and the mackerel pieces to the pan, together with half the chopped coriander. Simmer for 3–4 minutes until the fish is just cooked through. Sprinkle with the rest of the chopped coriander and serve with the cardamom rice.

SEARED CRAWFISH

with tomato, basil and lemon couscous

Crawfish, sometimes called spiny lobster or, wrongly, crayfish, are the big bruisers of the shellfish world. Unfortunately they are not that widely available, though you might hit it lucky in a good fish shop – but then comes the heart-stopping price. So unless you're a lottery winner, substitute lobster or raw tiger prawns.

Serves 4

2 × 900 g (2 lb) crawfish
250 ml (9 fl oz) Marinated Vegetable Stock
   (see page 179), Fish Stock (see page 180)
   or water
175 g (6 oz) couscous
6 Home-dried Tomatoes (see page 184),
   diced

3 tablespoons olive oil, plus extra for searing
   the crawfish and dressing the salad
juice of ½ lemon, plus 1 teaspoon
2 tablespoons chopped fresh basil
Maldon salt and freshly ground white pepper
25 g (1 oz) mixed salad leaves, such as frisée
   lettuce, dandelion, rocket and chives
50 ml (2 fl oz) Herb Oil (see page 186)

Drop the crawfish into a large pan of boiling water and cook for 8 minutes. Lift out, drop into a pan or sink full of cold water and leave to cool. Crack open the tail shells and carefully lift out the meat.

Bring the stock or water to the boil in a pan. Slowly pour in the couscous, give it a good stir and then add the tomatoes, the 3 tablespoons of olive oil, the juice of ½ a lemon and the basil. Cover, take off the heat and leave to stand for 5 minutes. Fluff up the grains with a fork and season to taste with some salt and pepper.

Cut the crawfish tail meat into about 16 medallions. Heat a little more olive oil in a large frying pan. When it is very hot, add the medallions a few at a time and sear for 1 minute on each side. Keep warm while you sear the rest.

Divide the couscous between 4 warmed serving plates (you can spoon it into a 7.5 cm (3 inch) pastry cutter to give it nice tower-shapes if you wish) and place the medallions around it.

Place the salad leaves in a bowl and dress with the rest of the lemon juice, a few drops of olive oil and some seasoning. Pile the leaves on top of the couscous, drizzle the herb oil around the edge of the plate and serve.

CRAB CAKES

with lobster mayonnaise and salad

I've made the mayonnaise with lobster oil for its intense flavour but, if you haven't got any or can't be bothered with the hassle of making it, this dish is still very tasty made with good-quality bought mayonnaise. Just add a crushed clove of garlic to the mix to help things along. You could use frozen or pasteurized crabmeat for the cakes but it's worth the effort to get fresh. The simplest and easiest way to do this is to buy crab claws only (without the body which is fiddly to shell) and ask the fishmonger to crack them for you.

Serves 4

juice of ½ lemon (about 1 ½ tablespoons)
450 g (1 lb) fresh white crabmeat
1 long, thin red chilli, finely chopped (seeds and all)
3 tablespoons chopped fresh coriander
Maldon salt and freshly ground white pepper
225 g (8 oz) fresh white breadcrumbs

sunflower oil for shallow frying
75 g (3 oz) baby salad leaves
a little olive oil

For the lobster mayonnaise:

1 medium farm-fresh egg yolk
1 tablespoon Dijon mustard
300 ml (10 fl oz) Lobster Oil (see page 187)
2 tablespoons warm water

First make the lobster mayonnaise. Mix the egg yolk and mustard together in a small bowl. Very gradually whisk in the lobster oil so that the mixture becomes thick and glossy. Spoon 4 tablespoons into another small bowl and stir in the warm water to thin it down into a sauce. Cover and set aside in the fridge.

For the crab cakes, put another 4 tablespoons of the mayonnaise into a bowl and whisk in the lemon juice. The rest of the mayonnaise can be stored in the fridge for 3–4 days. Fold in the crabmeat, chilli and the coriander and season to taste with salt and pepper. Form the mixture into eight 5 cm (2 inch) flat discs and then roll them in the breadcrumbs so that they take on a good, thick, even coating. Place them on a plate or tray, cover and chill for 1–2 hours to allow them to set.

When you are ready to cook the crab cakes, heat about 5 mm (¼ inch) sunflower oil in a large, heavy-based frying pan. Add the crab cakes and fry them for 3–4 minutes on each side until golden. Toss the salad leaves with a few drops of olive oil and some seasoning. Pile the salad leaves into the centres of 4 plates and place the crab cakes on top. Drizzle around the lobster mayonnaise and serve.

BAKED POTATOES

with spinach, Arbroath smokies and poached eggs

These are just posh baked tatties. If possible, use nice big floury potatoes such as Golden Wonder, Kerr's Pink, Cyprus or Maris Piper. The best bit about this dish is when you cut into the poached egg and the yolk runs down into the smoky, fishy potato filling. Tasty, very, very tasty – but slimming food this is not!

Serves 4

4 large floury baking potatoes, such as Golden Wonder, Kerr's Pink, Cyprus or Maris Piper
450 g (1 lb) Arbroath smokies
65 g (2½ oz) butter
275 g (10 oz) baby leaf spinach

Maldon salt and freshly ground black pepper
1 tablespoon chopped fresh chives
1 tablespoon chopped fresh flatleaf parsley
25 g (1 oz) Parmesan, finely grated
4 medium farm-fresh eggs
a few long-cut fresh chives, to garnish

Bake the potatoes at 190°C/375°F/Gas Mark 5 for 1½ hours. Meanwhile, skin and bone the smokies and break the flesh into small pieces.

When the potatoes are nearly ready, heat 15 g (½ oz) of the butter in a large pan. Add the spinach and stir-fry over a high heat for a few minutes until it has wilted into the bottom of the pan. Tip it into a colander and press out the excess water. Transfer to a chopping board, sprinkle with some salt and pepper and roughly chop.

Remove the potatoes from the oven and cut each one in half. Scoop out most of the flesh into a bowl, leaving behind enough to hold the skins in shape. Mash the potato with the rest of the butter and then stir in the flaked fish, chopped herbs and some seasoning. Divide the spinach between each potato shell and spread out with the back of a spoon. Cover with the potato mixture, flatten the tops and then sprinkle over the grated cheese and place on the rack of the grill pan.

Preheat the grill to high. Meanwhile, pour about 4 cm (1½ inches) water into a large frying pan and place it over a gentle heat. Slide the baked potatoes under the grill and cook for a few minutes until the cheese is golden and bubbling. As soon as little bubbles escape from the water in the frying pan, carefully break in the eggs and poach for 3 minutes, basting the top of the eggs with a little of the hot water as they cook. Lift them out with a slotted spoon and drain briefly on some kitchen paper. Place 2 baked potato halves on each plate, top with the poached eggs and garnish with a few chives.

POULTRY AND GAME

SWEET CHILLI CHICKEN KEBABS

Eating with your fingertips is a most underrated sensuous experience and barbecued kebabs are a most underrated dish. Here are four chances to redress the balance. You can thread the kebabs in advance for all these recipes.

These kebabs are quite spicy and, if you can stand the heat, they are great assembled with some extra pieces of seeded red chilli threaded onto the skewers along with the chicken. You can also serve them very simply with a fresh tomato and oregano salad and some thin, crisp French fries.

Serves 4

3 large chicken breasts, skinned and boned
2 small red onions
8 small, fresh bay leaves

For the sweet chilli marinade:
1 long, thin red chilli, seeded and very
  finely chopped

3 tablespoons olive oil
1½ tablespoons sweet red chilli sauce
2 teaspoons lemon juice
1 tablespoon chopped fresh oregano
1 clove garlic, crushed
Maldon salt and freshly ground black pepper

Remove any little fillets from the underside of each piece of chicken, then cut each breast lengthways into 4 long strips. Peel the onions, leaving the root ends intact. Cut each one into 6 thin wedges through the root so that the wedges stay together in one piece.

Mix together the ingredients for the marinade. Put the chicken, red onion wedges and bay leaves into a bowl, stir in the marinade and leave at room temperature for 2 hours or overnight in the fridge.

If you are going to barbecue your kebabs, allow about 40 minutes for the coals to reach the right temperature. If you are grilling your kebabs, preheat your grill to medium–high. Soak bamboo skewers, if using, for 30 minutes. Thread 3 strips of chicken alternately with 3 red onion wedges and 2 bay leaves onto four 25 cm (10 inch) metal or bamboo skewers. Cook on a barbecue or under a grill for 6–8 minutes, turning now and then, until cooked through but still nice and juicy.

MARJORAM AND LEMON CHICKEN KEBABS

with a tomato, basil and lemon pilaf

I've used chicken thighs in this recipe as I find the acidity of the lemon dries out breast meat too much. They're also tastier than breast meat and the extra fat bastes them during barbecuing, which is my favourite way of cooking them.

Serves 4

6 chicken thighs, skinned and boned

20 small cherry tomatoes

2 tablespoons chopped fresh marjoram

2 cloves garlic, crushed

finely grated zest and juice of 1 large lemon

3 tablespoons olive oil

Maldon salt and freshly ground black pepper

For the tomato, basil and lemon pilaf:

1 small onion, finely chopped

1–2 tablespoons olive oil

1 clove garlic, crushed

50 g (2 oz) sun-dried tomatoes in oil, drained
  and roughly chopped

275 g (10 oz) long-grain rice

300 ml (10 fl oz) tomato passata

300 ml (10 fl oz) Chicken Stock
  (see page 181)

finely grated zest of ½ small lemon

1 tablespoon lemon juice

3 tablespoons finely shredded fresh basil

Cut each chicken thigh into 4 pieces. Place in a bowl with all the other kebab ingredients, cover and leave to marinate at room temperature for 2 hours or in the fridge overnight.

Soak bamboo skewers, if using, for 30 minutes. If you are going to barbecue your kebabs, allow about 40 minutes for the coals to reach the right temperature. If you are grilling your kebabs, preheat your grill to medium–high after you have threaded the skewers.

For the pilaf, sauté the onion in the oil for 5 minutes until lightly browned. Add the garlic and fry for another minute. Stir in the sun-dried tomatoes and the rice and stir well so that all the grains of rice get nicely coated in the oil. Stir in the tomato passata and the stock, bring up to the boil, cover and cook over a low heat for 20 minutes. Meanwhile, thread 6 pieces of chicken and 5 cherry tomatoes alternately onto four 25 cm (10 inch) metal or bamboo skewers.

When the pilaf is half-way through cooking, cook the kebabs on the barbecue or under the grill for 6–8 minutes, turning now and then, until golden brown. Uncover the pilaf and fork in the lemon zest, lemon juice, basil and some salt and pepper to taste. Spoon the pilaf into the centre of 4 warmed plates and arrange the kebabs on top.

CHICKEN SATAY KEBABS

with spicy peanut sauce and Thai noodles

Another variation on the kebab theme, satay is great because the skewers can be threaded up in advance and kept on a tray, covered in clingfilm, until ready for cooking. Satay is now a widely appreciated flavour in this country, but the first time I tasted it was in the late 1970s in Singapore and I remember thinking it was the most exotic and delicious thing ever. I've tried many times to recapture that original flavour, but never quite got there. This comes pretty close, though.

Serves 4

6 large chicken breasts, skinned and boned

For the marinade:
1½ teaspoons cumin seeds
1½ teaspoons coriander seeds
½ teaspoon dried chilli flakes
1 large clove garlic, crushed
1 tablespoon light soy sauce
2 teaspoons light muscovado sugar
a good pinch of turmeric powder
50 ml (2 fl oz) canned coconut milk
1 tablespoon lime juice

For the spicy peanut sauce:
25 g (1 oz) natural roasted peanuts (that is, no added fat or salt)
3 cloves garlic, crushed
3 shallots, peeled and chopped
1 long, thin red chilli, seeded and chopped
2 teaspoons paprika
1½ tablespoons sunflower oil
175 ml (6 fl oz) canned coconut milk
1 tablespoon light muscovado sugar
½ teaspoon Maldon salt or to taste

For the Thai noodles:
75 g (3 oz) rice vermicelli (also known as stir-fry noodles)
juice of 1 lime
1 long, thin red chilli, seeded and finely chopped
6 spring onions, trimmed and thinly sliced
1 clove garlic, finely chopped
2 teaspoons sesame oil
2 teaspoons sunflower oil
1½ tablespoons Thai fish sauce
2 tablespoons chopped fresh coriander

Cut the chicken into 4 cm (1½ in) chunks. For the marinade, heat a dry, heavy-based frying pan until hot, add the cumin and coriander seeds and chilli flakes and toss around for a few seconds until they darken slightly and start to smell aromatic. Grind to a fine powder in a coffee grinder or with a pestle and mortar. Set aside 1 teaspoon for the sauce. Mix the rest with the remaining marinade ingredients in a bowl, stir in the chicken pieces and leave to marinate at room temperature for 2 hours or up to 24 hours in the fridge.

Shortly before you are about to cook the kebabs, soak the bamboo skewers, if using, for 10 minutes and make the spicy peanut sauce. Grind the peanuts to a fine powder and set them aside. Put the reserved cumin, coriander and chilli powder into a coffee grinder with the garlic, shallots, chopped chilli and paprika and whizz to a smooth paste. Heat the oil in a small pan, add the paste and cook over a medium heat for 3 minutes. Add the coconut milk, ground peanuts, sugar and salt, bring up to a gentle simmer and simmer for 2 minutes. Leave to cool slightly.

If you are going to barbecue your kebabs, allow about 40 minutes for the coals to reach the right temperature. If you are grilling your kebabs, preheat your grill to medium–high. Bring a large pan of lightly salted water to the boil. Thread the chicken pieces onto metal or pre-soaked bamboo skewers and cook for 8 minutes, turning them now and then, until lightly browned but still moist and juicy in the centre. Meanwhile, drop the noodles into the boiling water, take the pan off the heat and leave them to soak for 3 minutes. Drain them well, leave to cool slightly and then toss with the rest of the noodle ingredients.

Spoon the warm peanut sauce into 4 small dipping saucers or ramekins and serve with the kebabs and the noodles.

MOROCCAN CHICKEN KEBABS
with dates and bacon on a bed of spiced couscous

This final kebab variation looks to North Africa and the delightful sweet and spicy flavours found there. Do try and get fresh medjool dates, they taste so good.

Serves 4

4 chicken breasts, skinned and boned

2 tablespoons olive oil

1 tablespoon lemon juice

1 teaspoon ground cumin

1 teaspoon ground coriander

½ teaspoon turmeric powder

½ teaspoon paprika

½ teaspoon ground cinnamon

1 teaspoon soft light brown sugar

1 teaspoon harissa paste or minced red chilli
   from a jar

2 cloves garlic, crushed

12 fresh medjool dates

6 rashers rindless streaky bacon, cut in half

12 no-need-to-soak dried apricots

Maldon salt and freshly ground black pepper

For the spiced couscous:

3 tablespoons olive oil

1 medium onion, finely chopped

1 large clove garlic, finely chopped

1½ teaspoons ground cumin

1½ teaspoons ground coriander

1½ teaspoons ground paprika

½ teaspoon turmeric powder

350 ml (12 fl oz) Chicken Stock
   (see page 181)

225 g (8 oz) couscous

6 spring onions, trimmed and thinly sliced

2 long, thin red chillies, seeded and
   finely chopped

50 g (2 oz) toasted pine kernels

finely grated zest and juice of 1 lemon

1½ tablespoons chopped fresh coriander

1½ tablespoons chopped fresh mint

Cut the chicken into 4 cm (1½ inch) pieces. Place in a bowl with all the kebab ingredients except the dates, bacon and apricots and season with a little salt and pepper. Toss together well, cover and leave to marinate at room temperature for 2 hours or up to 24 hours in the fridge.

Soak bamboo skewers, if using, for 30 minutes. Make a slit in the side of each date and hook out the stones with the tip of a knife. Stretch each piece of bacon with the side of a kitchen knife and then wrap each one around a date. Thread the pieces of chicken, bacon-wrapped dates and apricots alternately onto 4 metal or bamboo skewers and set to one side.

If you are going to barbecue your kebabs, allow about 40 minutes for the coals to reach the right temperature. If you are grilling your kebabs, preheat your grill to medium–high. Cook the kebabs for 10–12 minutes, turning them every now and then, until the bacon is crisp and the chicken is cooked through but still moist and juicy in the centre. Keep the kebabs warm.

Next, prepare the couscous. Heat half the oil in a medium-sized pan. Add the onion and cook until it is soft and lightly browned. Add the garlic and cook for 1 minute, then stir in all the spices and fry for another minute. Add the stock and bring it to the boil. Pour in the couscous in a slow, steady stream, bring it up to the boil and stir once more. Cover, take the pan off the heat and set it aside for 5 minutes. Now uncover the pan and fork up the couscous into separate fluffy grains. Fork in the rest of the oil and the remaining couscous ingredients and season to taste with salt and pepper.

Spoon the couscous slightly off-centre onto 4 warmed plates and rest a kebab alongside each portion.

HARISSA CHICKEN

with couscous and lemon and cumin yoghurt

Harissa is a fiery red chilli paste from Morocco, but if you can't find it easily you can successfully substitute a minced red chilli paste which is available in all supermarkets now. This harissa coating will also work well on racks of lamb. Just roast them for 12–15 minutes. It will darken a little more than when you use it with chicken because there is no skin to protect it, but it will still taste just as good.

Serves 4

2 cloves garlic, crushed

1 tablespoon harissa paste or minced red chilli from a jar

2 tablespoons olive oil

45 g (1½ oz) sun-dried tomatoes in oil, very finely chopped

1 teaspoon chopped fresh thyme

Maldon salt and ½ teaspoon coarsely ground black pepper

4 large chicken suprêmes (that is, with the little wing bone still attached)

a little extra virgin olive oil, to serve

For the couscous:

2 medium onions, peeled and cut into wedges through the roots

2 red peppers, seeded and cut into quarters

4 tablespoons olive oil

a pinch of caster sugar

Maldon salt and freshly ground black pepper

2 teaspoons cumin seeds

2 teaspoons coriander seeds

¼ teaspoon fennel seeds

¼ teaspoon turmeric powder

2 cloves garlic, finely chopped

350 ml (12 fl oz) Chicken Stock (see page 181)

225 g (8 oz) couscous

50 g (2 oz) sultanas

50 g (2 oz) toasted pine kernels

3 tablespoons lemon juice

1 tablespoon chopped fresh oregano

1 tablespoon chopped fresh flatleaf parsley

For the lemon and cumin yoghurt:

1 tablespoon sunflower oil

1 teaspoon cumin seeds

6 tablespoons natural Greek or wholemilk yoghurt

finely grated zest of ½ small lemon

2 teaspoons lemon juice

a pinch of Maldon salt

Preheat the oven to 220°C/425°F/Gas Mark 7. For the couscous, mix the onion wedges, red peppers, 2 tablespoons of the olive oil, sugar and some seasoning together in a small roasting tin. Then prepare the chicken flavourings. Mix together the crushed garlic, harissa paste or minced red chilli, olive oil, sun-dried tomatoes, thyme, ½ teaspoon coarsely ground black pepper and a little salt. Loosen the skin of each chicken suprême, leaving it attached along one long edge, and spread the harissa mixture under the skin of each one in an even layer. Replace the skin and secure the open edge with a fine trussing skewer or a cocktail stick which has been soaked in cold water for 30 minutes. Place the chicken pieces in another small roasting tin.

Slide the tray of vegetables into the oven and roast for 10 minutes. Then slide the tray of chicken alongside and roast for a further 20–25 minutes.

Meanwhile, heat a dry, heavy-based frying pan over a high heat. Add the cumin, coriander and fennel seeds and dry-roast them until they darken slightly and start to smell aromatic. Grind them to a fine powder in a coffee grinder or with a pestle and mortar and then stir in the tumeric powder.

For the lemon and cumin yoghurt, heat the oil in a small pan. Add the cumin seeds and as soon as they start to pop, tip them into the yoghurt, add the lemon zest, lemon juice and salt and mix together well. Cover and leave in the fridge to chill.

Remove the chicken and vegetables from the oven. Leave the chicken somewhere warm to relax. Remove the skin from the pieces of red pepper and then cut them into small pieces together with the onions. Heat another tablespoon oil in a pan, add the chopped garlic and the ground, dry-roasted spices and fry for 30 seconds. Add the stock and bring to the boil. Stir in the couscous and the sultanas, bring back to the boil and remove from the heat. Cover and leave to steam for 5 minutes. Now fluff up the grains with a fork and fork in the rest of the oil, the roasted vegetables, pine kernels, lemon juice, chopped oregano and parsley and seasoning to taste.

Carve the chicken into diagonal slices. Spoon the couscous into the centres of 4 warmed plates and place the chicken on top. Spoon some of the cumin and yoghurt dressing around the edge of each plate and then drizzle around a little extra virgin olive oil.

ROAST PARTRIDGE

with garlic baby kale, deep-fried parsnip shreds and game gravy

I always tended to think of kale as animal feed, but the baby leaves stir-fried with garlic are just sublime – full of flavour and with a lovely crunchy texture. Partridge is one of my favourite game birds, in season from 1 September to 1 February; it has a paler flesh than most other game birds. If you haven't been shooting this weekend, guinea fowl makes a good substitute.

Serves 4

6 small, plump partridges
Maldon salt and freshly ground black pepper
1–2 tablespoons sunflower oil

For the game gravy:
1 tablespoon sunflower oil
4 small shallots, peeled and chopped
1 carrot, peeled and chopped
50 g (2 oz) mushrooms, sliced
1 clove garlic, crushed
1 fresh bay leaf
1 sprig of fresh thyme

6 white peppercorns, crushed
300 ml (10 fl oz) red or white wine
1 teaspoon redcurrant jelly
600 ml (1 pint) Chicken Stock (see page 181)
300 ml (10 fl oz) Beef Stock (see page 182)

For the deep-fried parsnip shreds:
sunflower oil for deep frying
2–3 small parsnips, peeled

For the garlic baby kale:
1 tablespoon sunflower oil
2 cloves garlic, cut into very fine shreds
450 g (1 lb) baby kale, washed and dried

First make the gravy. Remove the breasts from the partridges and remove the skin from each one. Cut the rest of the carcasses into small pieces. Heat the oil in a large pan, add the carcasses, shallots, carrot, mushrooms, garlic, bay leaf, thyme and peppercorns and fry over a high heat, stirring now and then, until everything is richly golden. Add the wine and boil until it has reduced to a couple of tablespoons. Add the redcurrant jelly and the chicken and beef stock and simmer until reduced to about 300 ml (10 fl oz). Strain through a sieve into a clean pan, pressing out as much liquid as you can with the back of a ladle. Taste the gravy and season with salt and a little more pepper if necessary. Set aside.

Preheat the oven to 230°C/450°F/Gas Mark 8. For the parsnip shreds, pour some oil into a medium-sized pan until it is about one-third full. Heat to 180°C/350°F. Meanwhile, peel each parsnip lengthways with a sharp potato peeler into long paper-thin strips, turning it every now and then, until you reach the hard central core, which you need to discard. As soon as the oil is ready,

drop in a handful of the parsnip shreds and fry for 1 minute until crisp and golden. Lift out with a slotted spoon and drain on kitchen paper. Repeat with the rest of the parsnip shreds.

Now it's time to cook the partridge breasts. Season them well on both sides with salt and pepper. Heat a flameproof, heavy-based frying pan until it is very hot. Add the oil and the partridge breasts and fry for 2 minutes on either side until richly golden. Turn the breasts rounded-side up, slide the pan into the oven and roast for 3 minutes until they are cooked but still slightly pink in the centre. Remove from the oven and leave somewhere warm to relax. Place the gravy over a low heat and leave to warm through.

For the kale, heat the oil in a wok or large pan, add the garlic and fry for a few seconds until it starts to colour. Add the kale and stir-fry over a high heat for about 1 minute. Remove the pan from the heat and season with salt and pepper. Spoon 3 small piles of the kale into the centres of 4 warmed plates. Place a partridge breast on top of each pile of kale. Spoon some of the gravy around the edge of each plate and then pile plenty of parsnip shreds in the centre.

PAN-FRIED PIGEON BREASTS

with baby bok choi and chilli and black bean sauce

This, for me, is a real fusion dish. Normally I would serve game with autumnal garnishes, such as cabbage, lentils, root vegetables or barley but, here the rich, meaty flavour goes really well with the Asian greens and the spicy chilli juices. And there's no complicated sauce to make either. This will definitely be on the menu at my new restaurant, Nairns, in Glasgow!

Serves 4

8 wood pigeon breasts, skinned
Maldon salt and freshly ground Sichuan
   peppercorns
5 tablespoons sunflower oil
350g (12 oz) baby bok choi
1 tablespoon light sesame oil
1 clove garlic, finely chopped
2.5 cm (1 inch) piece root ginger, peeled and
   finely chopped
2 tablespoons Chinese chilli and black
   bean sauce
1 tablespoon lime juice
4 tablespoons Chicken Stock (see page 181)
2 tablespoons chopped fresh coriander

Heat a large, heavy-based frying pan until it is very hot. Season the pigeon breasts with salt and Sichuan pepper, add to the pan with 1 tablespoon of the oil and fry for about 2 minutes on each side. Lift onto a plate, cover and leave somewhere warm to relax .

Trim the bok choi and cut each one in half through the stem. Add the sesame oil and the rest of the sunflower oil, garlic and ginger to the pan and fry for 1–2 minutes. Add the bok choi and stir-fry for 1 minute. Add the chilli and black bean sauce, lime juice, stock and chopped coriander and shake around for about 30 seconds.

Lift the bok choi out of the juices and pile into the centres of 4 warmed plates. Slice each pigeon breast thinly and lay on top of the bok choi. Taste the cooking juices left in the pan and season to taste. Spoon them around the edge of the plate and serve.

ROAST MEDALLIONS OF VENISON

with a confit of carrots and celery

To make a proper confit, you slow-braise meat or vegetables in duck fat. What I've done here is to slow-roast pieces of root vegetables in a little seasoned olive oil. To ensure even browning you need to stir and turn the vegetables several times during cooking. This process produces a richer and more intense flavour than conventional cooking methods, and the taste works particularly well with the rich flavour of game, making a perfect winter warmer.

Serves 6

6 × 150 g (5 oz) medallions of venison (bones
   and trimmings reserved for the jus)
Maldon salt and freshly ground white pepper
2 tablespoons olive oil

For the red wine jus:
5 tablespoons olive oil
4 sticks celery, roughly chopped
1 large onion, unpeeled and quartered
2 carrots, roughly chopped
1 head garlic, halved
4 shallots, roughly chopped
50 g (2 oz) mushrooms, roughly chopped
a sprig of fresh thyme

25 g (1 oz) butter
200 g (7 oz) can chopped tomatoes
½ bottle red wine
2 tablespoons rowan jelly

For the stovie potatoes:
6 × 100 g (4 oz) potatoes, preferably Golden
   Wonder
75 g (3 oz) butter

For the confit of carrots and celery:
6 carrots, peeled
4–6 sticks celery
2 tablespoons olive oil
1 clove garlic, finely chopped
1 tablespoon fresh thyme leaves

First make the red wine jus. Preheat the oven to 220°C/425°F/Gas Mark 7. Heat a large roasting tin on the top of the stove, add 3 tablespoons of the oil, the chopped up bones reserved from preparing the medallions, the celery, onion and carrots. Stir around over a high heat until they have turned a rich golden brown. Slide the tray into the oven and leave everything to roast for 30 minutes.

In a large stock pot, put the venison trimmings, garlic, shallots, mushrooms, thyme, the rest of the oil and the butter and cook over a medium–high heat for about 15 minutes until everything has caramelized nicely. Add the chopped tomatoes and the roasted bones and vegetables from the tin. Return the tin to the top of the stove, add the wine and deglaze by scraping up all the sticky

juices from the base. Pour the wine into the stock pot and boil rapidly until almost all of it has disappeared. Pour in enough water to cover the bones, and leave everything to simmer gently for 3 hours, lifting off any white frothy fat every now and then as it rises to the surface. Strain the stock through a colander first, skim off any fat and then pass it once more through a chinois or fine sieve into a clean pan. Add the rowan jelly and boil rapidly until the liquid has reduced to a well-flavoured, slightly syrupy jus. Set aside.

Lower the oven temperature to 180°C/350°F/Gas Mark 4. For the stovie potatoes, slice off either end of each one so that they are all the same size and look like little barrels when sitting upright. Spread the butter over the base of a small roasting tin or heavy-based, flameproof frying pan. Press in the potatoes, cut-side down, season well with salt and pepper and cook on top of the stove over a medium heat for about 15 minutes until golden brown. Turn them over, slide them into the oven and cook them for 1 hour.

For the confit of carrots and celery, cut both the vegetables diagonally into large 5 cm (2 inch) chunks. Heat a heavy-based pan over a high heat. Add 1 tablespoon of oil and the carrots and fry until they are golden brown. Transfer them to a roasting tin and repeat with the celery. Add the celery, garlic, thyme leaves and some seasoning to the carrots and set aside.

After the potatoes have been cooking for 40 minutes, season the medallions of venison on both sides with salt and pepper. Heat a heavy-based frying pan until very hot, add the oil and the medallions and fry the venison for 3–4 minutes on each side until nicely browned. Cover the pan with foil and set it aside somewhere warm for 15 minutes to allow the meat to relax. Five minutes later slide the carrots and celery into the oven and roast for 10 minutes. Season the red wine jus to taste and leave over a low heat to warm through.

To serve, place one potato and a large spoonful of the carrot and celery confit on each plate. Rest a medallion of venison on top of the confit and sprinkle with a little salt. Spoon the red wine jus around the edge of each plate.

ROAST LOIN OF HARE

on truffled spinach with horseradish mash and truffle oil

The flavour of truffle is one that I love but, unless you've just won the lottery, it's not one that many of us can afford. However, truffle oil, which is now stocked in some larger supermarkets, will give you the flavour without the cost. It's not as refined as the real thing but still lends a nice flavour. For the mashed potatoes, try to use fresh horseradish if you can get it, but jarred horseradish sauce (not the creamed one) will do. And, finally, you can serve venison instead of hare with these flavours equally well.

Serves 4

750 g (1½ lb) floury potatoes, such as Maris
   Piper or King Edward
40 g (1½ oz) unsalted butter
2 tablespoons horseradish sauce
Maldon salt and freshly ground white pepper
2½ tablespoons sunflower oil

4 hare loins, off the bone
900 g (2 lb) fresh spinach, washed and large
   stalks removed
2 teaspoons truffle oil, plus extra to serve
1 tablespoon olive oil
a little fresh black or white truffle, very finely
   diced (optional)

Peel the potatoes and cut them into chunks. Cook them in boiling salted water for 20 minutes or until tender.

Drain the potatoes and leave them in the colander until all the steam has disappeared. Drop them back into the pan and cook over a low heat for a few minutes to get rid of any more moisture. Mash them by hand, or pass them through a potato ricer or a large metal sieve, which will give you a very smooth mash. Beat in the butter and the horseradish sauce and season to taste with salt and pepper. Keep the mash warm over a low heat.

Heat a large frying pan until very hot. Add 2 tablespoons of the oil and the hare loins and fry over a high heat, turning now and then, until the meat is nicely browned on all sides. Transfer the loins to a tray, cover with foil and leave somewhere warm to relax while you cook the spinach. Heat the remaining sunflower oil in the same pan. Add the spinach and stir-fry over a high heat until it has wilted into the bottom of the pan. Tip into a colander and gently press out the excess water. Return the spinach to the pan with the truffle oil, olive oil and some salt and pepper and toss for a few seconds over a high heat. Remove from the heat and stir in the chopped truffles, if using.

Carve the loins of hare across into thin slices. Place piles of spinach slightly to one side on 4 warmed plates and overlap the slices of hare on top. Spoon a little of the horseradish mash alongside and serve garnished with some more of the truffle oil drizzled around the edge of the plate.

MEAT

SEARED LAMBS' LIVER
with bubble and squeak cake and shallot gravy

You can make the bubble and squeak cake in advance and reheat it, and the same with the gravy. Lambs' liver is often overlooked in favour of calves' liver but the former is just as tender and tasty as the calves' and half the price! It must be served slightly pink inside, otherwise it becomes tough, dry and tasteless.

Serves 4

sunflower oil

50 g (2 oz) Clarified Butter (see page 183),
   (optional)

8 thin slices lambs' liver, about 750 g (1½ lb)

4 tablespoons plain flour, seasoned with plenty
   of Maldon salt and freshly ground white
   pepper

For the bubble and squeak cake:

750 g (1½ lb) floury potatoes, such as Maris
   Piper or King Edward

15 g (½ oz) butter

1 large leek, cleaned and thinly sliced

175 g (6 oz) Savoy or other green cabbage,
   roughly chopped

sunflower oil for shallow frying

For the shallot gravy:

1½ tablespoons sunflower oil

1 onion, chopped

1 carrot, peeled and chopped

50 g (2 oz) mushrooms, sliced

1 fresh bay leaf

1 clove garlic, crushed

1 sprig of fresh thyme

6 white peppercorns, crushed

300 ml (10 fl oz) red or white wine

600 ml (1 pint) Chicken Stock (see page 181)

300 ml (10 fl oz) Beef Stock (see page 182)

Maldon salt and freshly ground white pepper

15 g (½ oz) butter

175 g (6 oz) shallots, peeled and thinly sliced

First make the gravy. You can do this well in advance if you wish. Heat 1 tablespoon of the oil in a large pan. Add the onion, carrot, mushrooms, bay leaf, garlic, thyme and peppercorns and fry over a high heat, stirring now and then, until everything is richly golden. Add the wine and boil until it has reduced to a couple of tablespoons. Add the chicken and beef stock and simmer until it has reduced to about 300 ml (10 fl oz). Strain through a sieve into a clean pan, pressing out as much liquid as you can with the back of a ladle. Taste the gravy and season with salt and more pepper if necessary. Set aside or chill until required.

For the bubble and squeak cake, peel the potatoes and cut them into large chunks. Cook them in boiling salted water for 15–20 minutes until tender. Drain and leave to go cold. Meanwhile, melt the butter in another pan. Add the sliced leek and fry for 4 minutes. Add the cabbage and 2 tablespoons of water, cover and cook over a medium–high heat, giving the pan a good shake every now and then, for 5 minutes. Tip the mixture into a bowl and leave it to go cold. Now crumble the potatoes into the bowl with the cabbage and leek, add plenty of seasoning to taste and mix together well.If you wish, you can do this ahead and leave all the vegetables to chill in the fridge overnight.

Heat a thin layer of oil in a 20 cm (8 inch) heavy-based frying pan – it must be flameproof as you will need to slide it into the oven later to finish the cooking. Add the bubble and squeak mixture and press it down well. Leave it to cook over a low heat for about 40 minutes until a good rich crust has formed over the bottom of the cake. Preheat the oven to 180°C/350°F/Gas Mark 4, slide in the pan and leave to cook for another 30 minutes.

While the bubble and squeak is in the oven, heat the rest of the oil and the butter for the gravy in a small pan. Add the sliced shallots and leave them to cook over a medium heat, stirring them every now and then, until they are soft and richly browned.

Just before you are ready to serve, add the fried shallots to the gravy and leave it over a medium heat to warm through. Heat a large, heavy-based frying pan until very hot. Add a little oil, and clarified butter if you wish, to the pan. Coat 2–3 slices of the liver in the seasoned flour, add to the hot pan and cook for just 1½ minutes on each side, until nicely browned on the outside but still slightly rare in the centre. (Don't be tempted to overcrowd the pan.) Lift each lot onto a baking tray as it cooks and keep it warm while you cook the rest.

To serve, turn the bubble and squeak cake out onto a board, cut it into 4 wedges and lift them onto 4 warmed serving plates. Place 2 slices of the liver on top of each wedge and spoon the shallot gravy around the edge of the plate.

CASEROLE OF SPICY MERGUEZ SAUSAGES

with beans, apples, bacon and cider

Merguez sausages come from North Africa and have a wonderful hot, spicy flavour. Casseroles such as this actually benefit from being made up a day or two before serving as the flavours get time to marry together and improve. This one also freezes well – just leave out the apples and add them to the pot when you reheat it (otherwise they'll turn to mush).

Serves 6

225 g (8 oz) mixed dried beans, such as
   haricot, red kidney, borlotti and
   black-eyed peas
900 g (2 lb) merguez or other spicy sausages
2 tablespoons olive oil
100 g (4 oz) bacon lardons (short chunky
   strips)
1 large onion, thinly sliced

2 cloves garlic, crushed
300 ml (10 fl oz) dry Normandy cider
450 ml (15 fl oz) Chicken Stock
   (see page 181)
3 fresh bay leaves
3–4 dessert apples
1 tablespoon softened butter
1 tablespoon plain flour
3 tablespoons chopped fresh parsley
Maldon salt and freshly ground black pepper

The day before you want to serve this dish, cover the beans in lots of cold water and leave them to soak overnight. The next day, bring a pan of water to the boil. Drain the beans, add them to the pan and bring them back to the boil. Boil them vigorously for 10 minutes and then drain once more and set aside.

Twist the sausages into 7.5–10 cm (3–4 inch) lengths. Heat 2 tablespoons of the oil in a large, heavy-based casserole dish or saucepan, add the sausages and fry them, turning them now and then, until they are nicely browned all round. Lift them out, cut into their shorter lengths and set to one side. Add the bacon lardons to the pan and fry for 3–4 minutes until golden brown. Add the onion and continue to fry until it is soft and lightly caramelized. Add the garlic and cook for 1 minute. Add the beans to the pan with the cider, chicken stock and the bay leaves, cover with a tight-fitting lid and leave to simmer for 1–1½ hours or until tender.

Quarter the apples, remove the cores and then peel. Cut them into thick slices, add to the pan with the browned sausages and cook for another 30 minutes.

Now you will only need to do the next step if your stew seems a little watery – and this will depend on the beans you've used and how fast they have been cooking. Blend the softened butter with the flour until smooth and then stir it into the stew and leave it to simmer gently for 5 minutes. Stir in the parsley, check the seasoning and serve in large soup plates with chunks of crusty fresh bread.

GRIDDLED PORK CHOPS
with oven-roasted vegetables and a tapenade dressing

The roast veggies for this dish can be cooked in advance and reheated, and the dressing can be made in advance and heated through at the last minute.

Serves 4

1 teaspoon fennel seeds
2 cloves garlic, crushed
120 ml (4 fl oz) olive oil
2 teaspoons lemon juice
Maldon salt and freshly ground white pepper
4 × 2.5 cm (1 inch) thick pork chops
2 small bulbs of Florence fennel
4 carrots, peeled and cut into 8 pieces
2 parsnips, peeled and cut into chunks

225 g (8 oz) small new potatoes, scrubbed
   clean if necessary
8 small whole cloves garlic, unpeeled
3 large sprigs of fresh rosemary, broken into
   short pieces

For the tapenade dressing:

1 tablespoon tapenade (black olive paste)
50 ml (2 fl oz) extra virgin olive oil
1 tablespoon balsamic vinegar
1 tablespoon chopped fresh sage and
   fennel herb

Preheat the oven to 220°C/425°F/Gas Mark 7. Grind the fennel seeds in a mortar with the garlic, 2 tablespoons of the olive oil, the lemon juice and some seasoning to make a coarse paste. Rub over the surface of the pork chops and set aside at room temperature.

Trim the bulbs of fennel but leave the root ends intact. Cut each bulb into wedges through the root so that each wedge stays together in one piece. Put all the vegetables and the unpeeled cloves of garlic into a roasting tin with the rest of the olive oil and plenty of seasoning. Toss well and then spread into an even layer. Tuck in the sprigs of rosemary and roast the vegetables for 45 minutes, turning them every so often as they brown, until they are golden and tender.

Shortly before the vegetables are ready, put the tapenade, olive oil, vinegar and some seasoning into a small pan. Heat a ridged, cast-iron griddle over a high heat. Brush it with some oil, add the pork chops and cook for 4–5 minutes on each side until they are attractively marked in lines and cooked through but still moist and juicy in the centre. (There is nothing worse than dry, overcooked pork.) Then tip them on their fatty edges and cook for a couple of minutes until the fat is nice and crisp. Lift them onto a baking tray and keep warm.

Place the pan of tapenade dressing over a very low heat and leave it to just warm through. Remove the roasted vegetables from the oven and slide the cooked garlic cloves out of their skins. Season with a little more salt and pepper if necessary. Pile the vegetables into the centres of 4 warmed plates and rest a griddled pork chop on top of each pile. Stir the chopped herbs into the dressing and spoon a little around the outside of each plate.

WARM MUTTON SALAD

with olive oil croûtons

Warm salads were much in vogue a couple of years ago, but seem to have fallen out of favour in recent times. This is a bit of a shame as they are relatively quick to throw together, and right up there in the taste league. Mutton is lamb which is more than a year old, and it has a deeper, more mature flavour than a young beast. The down side is that it can be a bit chewy if it isn't hung properly, so make sure you carve it as thinly as possible. Remember to add any juices released during carving to the salad.

Serves 4

100 g (4 oz) baby new potatoes
1 × 350 g (12 oz) fillet of mutton or lamb
Maldon salt and freshly ground white pepper
4 tablespoons olive oil
1 tablespoon good-quality balsamic vinegar
1 head frisée lettuce, washed and separated
    into small tendrils
1 red or yellow pepper, seeded and finely diced
Tomatoes Concassées (see page 184),
    use 2 tomatoes

1 carrot, peeled and grated
25 g (1 oz) pitted black olives
25 g (1 oz) Parmesan shavings
small bunch of fresh chives, cut into 5 cm
    (2 inch) lengths

For the croûtons:
½ loaf stale French bread
2 tablespoons olive oil
1 clove garlic, crushed

First cook the potatoes in boiling salted water for 10–15 minutes until just tender. Drain and leave to cool. Then make the croûtons. Tear the bread into small, bite-sized chunks. Heat a heavy-based frying pan until quite hot, add the oil, the garlic and the bread and toss over a high heat for about 5 minutes until crisp and golden brown. Remove the croûtons from the pan and drain on kitchen paper. Keep them warm. Slice the cooked potatoes and add them to the same pan with a drizzle more oil, if needed. Fry until brown and crispy on both sides. Set aside with the croûtons.

Season the mutton or lamb fillet with salt and pepper. Heat the frying pan until very hot, add 2 tablespoons of oil and the mutton or lamb and sear on each side for about 2 minutes. Take the pan off the heat, lift the meat onto a plate and set aside to relax in a warm place for a few minutes.

Return the pan to the heat and deglaze with the vinegar, making sure that you scrape up all the crusty bits from the bottom of the pan. Add the remaining oil and season to taste with salt and pepper. Put the lettuce, pepper, tomatoes, carrot and olives together in a bowl, toss and season. Carve the mutton or lamb into thin slices across the length of the loin. Add the slices to the salad and then pour over the juices from the pan. Add the potatoes, toss once more and divide between 2 plates. Sprinkle over the croûtons and garnish with the Parmesan and chives.

SCOTTISH ALE-BRAISED OXTAIL

with butter beans

This rustic stew is cooked over a two-day period, which gives time for the meat to become unbelievably tender and enables you to get rid of all the excess fat from the sauce before adding the vegetables and beans. It is nice served in a large tureen. All you need is a big bowl of mash to go with it – and more beer!

Serves 6

2 oxtails, together weighing about 2 kg
    (4½ lb), cut into 5 cm (2 inch) pieces
50 g (2 oz) flour with 1 teaspoon Maldon salt
    and plenty of freshly ground black pepper
4 tablespoons olive oil
1 large onion, chopped
600 ml (1 pint) Scottish dark ale (or Irish stout
    if you must)
450 ml (15 fl oz) Beef Stock (see page 182)
3 cloves garlic, crushed

1 bouquet garni of fresh bay leaves and thyme
Maldon salt and freshly ground black pepper
350 g (12 oz) button onions
50 g (2 oz) butter
4 sticks celery, sliced
350 g (12 oz) carrots, peeled and sliced
2 × 400 g (14 oz) cans butter beans or other
    white beans, drained and rinsed
1 clove garlic, very finely chopped
2 tablespoons fresh white breadcrumbs
2 tablespoons chopped fresh flatleaf parsley

Trim any excess fat off the oxtail and toss it in the seasoned flour. Heat 2 tablespoons of the oil in a large, flameproof casserole. Fry the oxtail a few pieces at a time on all sides until richly browned. Remove to a plate and set aside.

Add another tablespoon of oil to the pan with the onion and cook over a medium heat, stirring now and then, for 10 minutes or until soft and nicely browned. Stir in any leftover seasoned flour and cook for 1 minute. Take the pan off the heat and gradually stir in the ale and beef stock. Return the oxtail to the pan with the crushed garlic and the bouquet garni, season with a little salt and pepper, cover and simmer for 3 hours, turning the pieces of oxtail over from time to time. Now cover loosely, leave to cool and then refrigerate overnight.

The next day lift the layer of fat off the top of the casserole and discard. Place the oxtail over a gentle heat and bring slowly up to the boil. Meanwhile, fry the button onions in the remaining oil until well browned. Add half the butter, the celery and carrots and fry for 3 minutes. Add these vegetables and the butter beans to the casserole and simmer uncovered for about 30 minutes, by which time the oxtail and the vegetables should be tender. Remove the bouquet garni.

Heat the rest of the butter in a clean frying pan. Add the garlic and the breadcrumbs and fry, stirring continuously, until they are crisp and golden brown. Take the pan off the heat and stir in the parsley and some seasoning. Sprinkle the crumbs over the surface of the oxtail and serve.

TWICE-COOKED SOY-BRAISED PORK

with stir-fried Chinese leaves and steamed rice

The 'twice-cooked' refers to the pork first being simmered for a long, slow cook to make it really tender and so that it absorbs all the added flavours. The second cooking is hot and fast to crisp up the fat and give the meat a crispy crust. Plain steamed rice is all this dish needs as an accompaniment as there's so much flavour in the meat and the sauce.

Serves 4

900 g (2 lb) unskinned, boned belly pork in
  one piece
150 ml (5 fl oz) dark soy sauce, plus
  2 tablespoons for sauce
150 ml (5 fl oz) dry sherry
1 long, thin red chilli, halved
4 cloves garlic
6 cm (2½ inch) piece root ginger, peeled
  and sliced
2 star anise
sunflower oil for frying

1½ tablespoons hoisin sauce
1 teaspoon sugar
275 g (10 oz) long-grain rice
a pinch of Maldon salt
4 spring onions, cut into long, thin shreds

For the stir-fried Chinese leaves:

450 g (1 lb) Chinese leaves
2 tablespoons sunflower oil
2.5 cm (1 inch) piece root ginger, peeled and
  finely chopped
1 long, thin red chilli, seeded and very finely
  chopped

Bring 2.25 litres (4 pints) of water to the boil in a large pan. Add the piece of belly pork, 150 ml (5 fl oz) soy sauce, the sherry, red chilli, 2 cloves of garlic, two-thirds of the sliced root ginger and the star anise. Bring back to the boil and leave to simmer very gently for about 2 hours until the pork is meltingly tender.

Remove the pork from the pan to a plate and leave to cool. Strain the stock, reserving 150 ml (5 fl oz) for the sauce. The rest can either be saved for soup or frozen.

For the sauce, very finely chop the remaining ginger and garlic. Heat ½ tablespoon of sunflower oil in a small pan. Add the ginger and garlic and stir-fry until lightly golden. Add the reserved stock, the 2 tablespoons soy sauce, the hoisin sauce and the sugar and leave to simmer until reduced and well flavoured. Keep the sauce warm.

Rinse the rice under cold water until the water runs clear. Put the rice into a pan with 600 ml (1 pint) water and the salt. Bring to the boil and boil for 1 minute. Cover and leave to simmer gently for 10 minutes. Then take the pan off the heat, with the lid in place, and leave to steam undisturbed for another 10 minutes.

Meanwhile, pour about 2.5 cm (1 inch) of sunflower oil into a large pan and heat it to 180°C/350°F. While it is coming up to temperature, cut the piece of pork into 4 neat, squared-off pieces and dry them well on kitchen paper. Also, cut the Chinese leaves into 2.5 cm (1 inch) wide strips. Deep-fry the pieces of pork for 4 minutes until crisp and golden – take care, because as the skin crisps up, the fat tends to spit quite a lot. The bigger and deeper the pan you can use, the better. Drain the pork on kitchen paper and slide into a warm oven to keep crisp.

Now cook the Chinese leaves. Heat the oil in a wok or another large pan. Add the ginger and red chilli and stir-fry for a few seconds. Add the Chinese leaves and stir-fry for 2–3 minutes.

Cut each piece of pork across into 5 mm (¼ inch) thick slices. Spoon some steamed rice slightly to one side on 4 plates and arrange overlapping slices of the pork on the outermost sides of the rice. Pile the stir-fried Chinese leaves on the other side of the plates. Skim any fat off the surface of the sauce, spoon the sauce around the edge of each plate and serve, garnished with the shredded spring onions.

ROAST MARINATED LOIN OF LAMB
with basil potatoes

A perfect example of the motto 'the simpler the better'. If you are lucky enough to get your hands on some good, native new season's lamb, then this recipe is all you need for a truly tasty dish. No fancy sauces or garnishes needed here, just a nice piece of perfectly cooked marinated meat and some new potatoes in buttery basil juices. The meat needs to be marinated a couple of days in advance for maximum flavour and, to finish it off, all you have to do is fling it in the frying pan for a few minutes.

Serves 4

5 tablespoons olive oil
2 cloves garlic, crushed
leaves from 2 sprigs of fresh rosemary
450g (1 lb) loin of lamb, trimmed but with the
    skin still on
freshly ground black pepper
450 g (1 lb) new potatoes
Maldon salt
25 g (1 oz) fresh basil leaves
50 g (2 oz) butter

Put 3 tablespoons of the olive oil, the garlic and the rosemary leaves into a small dish, just large enough to take the lamb. Add the loin, season with about 12 turns of the black-pepper mill and then turn it over in the mixture so that it gets well coated. Cover and set aside to marinate for 4–5 hours at room temperature or, better still, for 12–36 hours in the fridge, giving the loin a turn every now and then in the marinade.

When you are ready, cook the potatoes in boiling salted water for 20–25 minutes until tender. Meanwhile, lift the lamb out of the marinade and pick off any bits of garlic and rosemary as they will burn. Season the meat with salt. Heat a frying pan until it is very hot. Add the lamb and the rest of the oil and cook for 3 minutes on each side until the meat is nicely browned on the outside but still pink in the centre. Remove the pan from the heat and set it aside somewhere warm for 10 minutes to allow the meat to relax.

Finely chop the basil. Drain the potatoes and return them to the pan with the butter, basil and a pinch of salt and pepper. Toss together well. Carve the lamb across into thin slices. Divide the potatoes between 4 warmed plates and place some of the lamb on top. Spoon the buttery juices left in the potato pan around the edges of the plates and serve.

SPICED LAMB BALLS

Mincing the lamb allows you to use a cheaper cut, such as foreleg or neck, as well as allowing the spices to permeate the meat. Cooking the mince in the tomato sauce ensures a real exchange of tastes between the meat and the sauce. This is the kind of dish which improves by being made beforehand so that the flavour matures and intensifies, making it an easy and ideal dish for a dinner party. Simply reheat it before plonking it down on the table in a nice casserole dish and serving it with plain boiled rice, pasta or new potatoes. A crisp green salad wouldn't go amiss either.

Serves 4

450 g (1 lb) minced lamb

2 cloves garlic, crushed

1 tablespoon Worcestershire sauce

2 tablespoons chopped fresh oregano

2 teaspoons ground cumin

1 long, thin red chilli, finely diced (seeds and
   all if you like the heat)

4 tablespoons chopped fresh flatleaf parsley

1 medium farm-fresh egg

Maldon salt and freshly ground black pepper

2 tablespoons olive oil

For the tomato and aubergine sauce:

1 medium onion, finely chopped

1 clove garlic, crushed

3 tablespoons olive oil

1 long, thin red chilli, finely chopped

1 aubergine, cut into 1 cm (½ inch) dice

400 g (14 oz) can chopped tomatoes

2 tablespoons tomato ketchup

2 tablespoons chopped fresh basil

For the meatballs, put all the ingredients except the oil in a bowl and season with 1 teaspoon of salt and 20 turns of the black-pepper mill. Mix together well and then shape into balls slightly larger than golfballs. Heat the oil in a large pan. Add the balls (in batches, if necessary, because you want them to brown nicely) and fry them until they are well coloured all over. Lift them onto a baking sheet and set aside.

For the sauce, add the onion and garlic to the pan and fry for 5–7 minutes until soft. Add the rest of the oil, the chilli and the diced aubergine (it will absorb lots of oil while cooking) and fry until soft and starting to brown. Now add the tomatoes, ketchup and some seasoning and leave the sauce to simmer gently for 20 minutes.

Add the meatballs to the sauce and simmer for another 15 minutes. Stir in the basil, season to taste with salt and pepper and serve with pasta or plain boiled rice.

VEGETARIAN

CHEESE AND TOMATO SALSA TORTILLAS
with soured cream and salad

In Mexico they fill tortillas (very thin, round, unleavened breads) with almost anything – meat sauces, strips of chicken, refried beans, cheese… Here I have deep-fried some Italian mozzarella cheese in a crispy coating, then rolled it up inside the breads with some soured cream and chilli salsa to make a very tasty and substantial lunch or supper dish. If you can't be bothered to make the tortillas – although home-made ones are very easy and much flakier and tastier than ready-made ones – you can buy them from the supermarket instead. But make sure you buy flour tortillas and not those brittle, bright yellow, U-shaped corn ones.

Serves 6

sunflower oil for deep frying
350 g (12 oz) mozzarella (about 3 balls)
Maldon salt and freshly ground black pepper
25 g (1 oz) plain flour
2 medium farm-fresh eggs, beaten
75 g (3 oz) fresh white breadcrumbs
150 ml (5 fl oz) soured cream
100 g (4 oz) mixed baby salad leaves
3 teaspoons extra virgin olive oil
1 teaspoon lime juice

For the tortillas:
350 g (12 oz) plain flour
1½ teaspoons Maldon salt
75 g (3 oz) lard or white vegetable fat
175 ml (6 fl oz) warm water

For the tomato salsa:
8 tomatoes, skinned, seeded and diced
1 red onion, finely chopped
2 green chillies, seeded and chopped
juice of 1 lime
3 tablespoons chopped fresh coriander

For the tortillas, sift the flour and salt into a bowl. Add the fat and rub together into very fine crumbs. Slowly pour in enough warm water, stirring with a small palette knife, to make a soft dough. Work it together into a ball with your hands, transfer it to a lightly floured surface and knead for 3 minutes until smooth. Rub the ball of dough lightly with flour, slip it into a plastic bag and seal. Leave to rest for 1 hour.

Knead the dough once more for a minute and then leave it to rest for another 10 minutes. Pinch off 45 g (1½ oz) pieces of the dough, roll them into neat balls and then flatten them slightly with the palm of your hand. (You should have enough for 12 tortillas.) Dust the work surface, the top of the dough and the rolling pin with flour and then roll out each flattened ball very thinly into an 18 cm (7 inch) circle, dusting everything with a little more flour now and then to prevent sticking.

Heat a smooth, cast-iron griddle or heavy-based frying pan over a high heat until very hot. Add a tortilla and cook it for 20 seconds on one side. Flip it over and cook for another 10 seconds and then continue to turn it every 10 seconds until the dough is cooked through and the tortilla is covered on both sides with golden-brown spots. This should take a total of about 1 minute. Repeat with the rest of the tortillas, stack them on a plate and leave them to cool. Divide them into stacks, wrap them in foil and reheat them in a warm oven for a couple of minutes just before you are ready to serve.

Mix together all the ingredients for the salsa and set aside. Pour some oil into a large pan so that it is about one-third full and heat it to 190°C/375°F. Cut the cheese into 1 × 6 cm (½ × 2½ inch) fingers and dry them off on some kitchen paper. Season them with a little salt and then dip them first into the flour, then the eggs and finally the breadcrumbs. Deep-fry a few pieces at a time for 1–1½ minutes until crisp and golden brown. Lift out with a slotted spoon onto a tray lined with kitchen paper and leave to drain for a minute.

To serve, spoon some of the tomato salsa down the centre of each tortilla and top with some of the deep-fried cheese. Spoon over a little of the soured cream, roll up and place 2 side by side on 4 serving plates. Toss the salad leaves with the oil, lime juice and a little seasoning. Pile them in the centre of the tortillas and serve.

RÖSTI

with spinach, poached farm eggs and mustard hollandaise

Very simple, very eggy, very good. As with all straightforward dishes the raw ingredients are of prime importance and this means good roasting spuds, preferably Golden Wonder, Maris Piper or other potatoes with a high potato mass (which makes them feel heavy) and low sugar content. The spinach should have thick leaves with the biggest stalks removed – tedious I know, but worth it. That leaves the eggs, which make this dish sing. What we need here are farm eggs, *real* free-range eggs from a proper farm, not the so-called free-range eggs from factory farms where the chickens only get to glimpse daylight every now and then. So make an effort to find a farm which has a few chickens grubbing about in the yard and pay good cash for a real treat. If you can get them, not only do they taste sublime (with deeply coloured, almost orange, yolks) but they keep their shape much better when poached.

Serves 4

1 tablespoon sunflower oil

450 g (1 lb) leaf spinach, washed and drained

15 g (½ oz) butter

Maldon salt and freshly ground white pepper

4 farm-fresh eggs

coarsly crushed black peppercorns, to garnish

For the rosti potatoes:

2 × 225 g (8 oz) potatoes, such as Golden Wonder, Maris Piper or Cyprus

4 teaspoons olive oil

50 g (2 oz) Clarified Butter (see page 183)

For the mustard hollandaise:

175 g (6 oz) butter

3 medium farm-fresh egg yolks

1 teaspoon Dijon mustard

First make the rösti potatoes. Peel the potatoes and coarsely grate them into a bowl. Season with ½ teaspoon of salt and some pepper. Heat half the oil and half the butter in one 20 cm (8 inch) heavy-based frying pan or 4 individual 12.5 cm (5 inch) blini pans. Add the potato mix and press it down evenly with the back of a spatula. Fry over a low–medium heat for about 15 minutes until you can see traces of colour at the edges – but take care not to cook it over too high a heat or it will over-brown before the potato on the inside has had a chance to cook. Cover the pan(s) with an inverted plate, hold the two together and turn over so that the rösti is transferred to the plate. Heat the remaining oil and butter in the pan. Slide the rösti back in on its uncooked side and cook for another 10–15 minutes until golden. Now you can either keep the rösti warm, or leave to cool and reheat later in the oven at 180°C/350°F/Gas Mark 4 for 5 minutes.

For the mustard hollandaise, melt the butter in a small pan and keep it hot. Put the yolks and mustard into a large, heatproof bowl, add 1 tablespoon of hot water and rest the bowl over a pan of barely simmering water. Whisk for 3–4 minutes until the mixture becomes pale, thick and moussey. Then gradually whisk in the butter, a tablespoon at a time, taking care not to let the mixture get too hot or it will curdle. Take the bowl off the heat and whisk in a couple of pinches of salt and 8 turns of the pepper mill. Keep the sauce warm while you cook the eggs and the spinach – a clever trick is to fill a Thermos flask with hot water, drain it and dry it well. Pour in the hollandaise and seal the flask. It will keep warm for ages.

For the spinach, heat the oil in a large pan, add the spinach and stir-fry over a high heat until it wilts into the bottom. Tip it into a colander, gently press out the excess liquid and then return it to the pan and toss with the butter and some seasoning. Keep it warm.

To poach the eggs, pour 3.5 cm (1½ inches) of boiling water into a clean frying pan and place it over a low heat – the water should show a few bubbles on the base of the pan, but no more. Break the eggs carefully into the hot water and cook for 3 minutes, basting the tops of the eggs with a little of the hot water as they cook. Lift them out of the water with a slotted spoon and drain on kitchen paper.

To serve, cut the large potato rösti into quarters and lift one piece onto each plate, or place the individual röstis in the centres of 4 plates. Spoon on some of the spinach, add a poached egg and then spoon over some of the hollandaise. Sprinkle with a little of the coarsely crushed black peppercorns and serve immediately.

BAKED GNOCCHI

with wild mushrooms, garlic and Parmesan

This really proves that you don't need to have meat with every meal. Without the mushrooms, this dish is known as gnocchi alla romana and is essentially a thick mixture of Parmesan-flavoured polenta, set in a tray and then cut into pieces and baked in the oven until crisp and golden. Layered with a mixture of wild mushrooms and topped with a crisp crust of more cheese and breadcrumbs, it turns into something that even the meat-eaters will fight over.

Serves 4

1 litre (1¾ pints) water
225 g (8 oz) quick-cook polenta
50 g (2 oz) Parmesan, finely grated
1 farm-fresh egg yolk
a pinch of freshly grated nutmeg
2 tablespoons melted butter

Maldon salt
3 tablespoons olive oil
450 g (1lb) mixed wild mushrooms, wiped
* clean and hard stalks removed*
2 cloves garlic, crushed
10 g (¼ oz) fresh white breadcrumbs
1 tablespoon chopped fresh parsley

Bring the water to the boil in a large pan. Reduce the heat and then slowly whisk in the polenta, making sure that you don't get any lumps. Leave it to cook over a very low heat for 10 minutes, whisking it frequently, until it becomes thick and comes away from the sides of the pan. Take the pan off the heat and stir in 40 g (1½ oz) of the Parmesan, the egg yolk, nutmeg, 1 tablespoon of the melted butter and salt to taste. Pour the mixture into a lightly greased 23 × 33 cm (9 × 13 inch) Swiss roll tin and spread it out with a wet palette knife so that the mixture is level and no more than 1 cm (½ inch) thick. Cover and chill for at least 2 hours or overnight.

Preheat the oven to 200°C/400°F/Gas Mark 6. Cut the polenta mixture into 24 small squares and set to one side. Heat the oil in a large, deep frying pan. Cut the mushrooms where necessary into thick slices, add to the pan with the garlic and fry over a high heat for about 3 minutes.

Arrange overlapping squares of the gnocchi and mushrooms in lines in a well-buttered 20 × 28 cm (8 × 11 inch) shallow, ovenproof dish. Mix the rest of the melted butter with the breadcrumbs, stir in the rest of the Parmesan and the tablespoon of chopped parsley and sprinkle over the top of the dish. Bake in the oven for 25–30 minutes until crisp and golden. Serve immediately.

STICKY RICE TEMPURA
with avocado and mango salsa, herb salad and soy vinaigrette

This takes the sushi rice idea one step further by enclosing it in a crispy tempura batter and serving it with a salsa on top and a few dressed leaves. Make up the salsa in advance (without the coriander), then make the rice patties and deep-fry them at the last moment.

Serves 6

375 g (13 oz) Japanese sticky rice
600 ml (1 pint) water
2 tablespoons caster sugar
1 teaspoon Maldon salt
4 tablespoons rice vinegar
sunflower oil for deep frying
1 teaspoon wasabi paste

For the avocado and mango salsa:

1 ripe but firm mango
1 ripe but firm avocado
1 small red onion, finely diced
1 long, thin red chilli, finely diced (seeds and
   all if you like the heat)
finely grated zest and juice of 1 lime
2 tablespoons Japanese pickled ginger,
   drained and cut into fine shreds
2 tablespoons olive oil
½ teaspoon Maldon salt
freshly ground white pepper
4 tablespoons chopped fresh coriander

For the soy vinaigrette:

2 tablespoons good-quality soy sauce
150 ml (5 fl oz) best-quality olive oil
1 teaspoon Dijon mustard
2 tablespoons lime juice
1 teaspoon clear honey

For the tempura batter:

50 g (2 oz) self-raising flour
50 g (2 oz) cornflour
ice-cold sparkling mineral water

For the herb salad:

a handful of mixed coriander, chervil and
   chive sprigs
a few drops of olive oil
½ teaspoon lime juice

For the sticky rice tempura, put the rice into a sieve and wash it under running cold water, working your fingers through the grains until the water runs clear. Drain the rice and put it into a pan with the water. Bring it quickly to the boil, then the heat turn down very low and cook for 10 minutes. Remove from the heat, cover and leave undisturbed for 10 minutes. This timing is crucial to produce the correct consistency for the sticky rice.

Stir the sugar and salt into the vinegar until dissolved. Turn the rice out into a bowl and stir in the vinegar mixture, fanning the rice as you do so to cool it and produce a sheen on it. Divide the rice mixture into 6 and shape into small 10 cm (4 inch) patties. Cover and leave in the fridge for 2 hours to set.

For the avocado and mango salsa, peel the mango and then slice the flesh away from either side of the flat stone in 2 whole pieces. Cut into small, neat dice. Cut the avocado in half and remove the stone. You can do this by whacking the stone with a sharp knife so that the blade grips it. Give a gentle twist and the stone will come out very easily. Cut the avocado into quarters, peel off the skin and cut the flesh into small dice the same size as the mango. Mix in a bowl with the rest of the salsa ingredients, cover and leave to marinate at room temperature for at least 1 hour.

Meanwhile, make the soy vinaigrette. Simply whisk all the ingredients together and set aside until you are ready to serve.

Shortly before serving, pour some sunflower oil into a pan until it is about one-third full and heat it to 180°C/350°F. Smear one side of each rice cake with some of the wasabi paste. Make the tempura batter by sifting the flour and cornflour into a bowl. Mix in enough water (make sure it is ice-cold) with a fork to make a slightly lumpy batter with the consistency of single cream. Dip the rice cakes in the batter and fry 2 at a time until crisp and lightly golden – about 4 minutes. Lift them out with a slotted spoon onto some kitchen paper and leave to drain while you cook the rest.

Place a rice cake in the centre of a plate. Spoon some of the salsa into a 5 cm (2 inch) plain pastry cutter and press down lightly. Using a fish slice or a palette knife, carefully lift the salsa onto the centre of the rice cake and remove the cutter. Repeat for the rest of the cakes. For the herb salad, toss the herb sprigs with the oil and lime juice and pile on top. Put the soy vinaigrette in a small bowl and serve separately.

AUBERGINE FRITTER STACKS

with crème fraîche raita and curry oil

The combination of these crispy aubergine wafers and the fresh and spicy tomato sauce, flecked with coriander, makes a delicious vegetarian starter too.

Serves 4

2 medium aubergines, peeled and
    coarsely grated
Maldon salt and freshly ground black pepper
175 g (6 oz) chickpea flour
1 tablespoon ground coriander
2 teaspoons ground cumin
½ teaspoon turmeric powder
½ teaspoon cayenne pepper
1 tablespoon sunflower oil, plus extra for
    shallow frying
1½ tablespoons lemon juice
175 ml (6 fl oz) warm water
2 medium farm-fresh egg whites

1 quantity Crème Fraîche Raita (see page 50)
a little Curry Oil (see page 187), to serve

For the tomato sauce:
2 tablespoons olive oil
1 medium onion, very finely chopped
1 large clove garlic, crushed
1 long, thin red chilli, finely chopped, seeds
    and all
1 × 400 g (14 oz) can chopped tomatoes
2 tablespoons tomato ketchup
1 sprig of fresh thyme
1 fresh bay leaf
2 tablespoons chopped fresh coriander
Maldon salt and freshly ground black pepper

Mix the aubergines with 1 teaspoon of salt and set aside in a sieve to drain. Sift the chickpea flour, spices and 1 teaspoon of salt together into a bowl. Make a well and add 1 tablespoon sunflower oil, the lemon juice and water and stir together. Beat well with an electric whisk to make a smooth batter and set aside for 30 minutes. Meanwhile, make the tomato sauce. Heat the oil in a pan, add the onion, garlic and chilli and fry for 5 minutes until soft but not coloured. Add the tomatoes, ketchup, thyme and bay leaf and leave to simmer for 30 minutes until quite thick.

Rinse the aubergines under cold water to remove the excess salt and then squeeze well, first in your hands and then in a clean tea towel. Stir them into the batter. Whisk the egg whites with a pinch of salt into soft peaks and gently fold them into the batter. Pour about 1 cm (½ inch) of sunflower oil into a large frying pan. Drop in large spoonfuls of the aubergine batter, spacing them a little apart, and fry for 3–4 minutes on each side over a medium heat until golden. Drain on kitchen paper and keep warm while you cook the rest. You should have 12 fritters in total.

To serve, stir the coriander into the sauce and season to taste with salt and pepper. Place one fritter in the centre of a warmed plate and cover with a spoonful of the sauce. Cover with another fritter, some more sauce and then a third fritter. Pile the crème fraîche raita on top of the last fritter and drizzle a little curry oil around the edge of the plate.

CHANTERELLE MUSHROOM RISOTTO

with Parmesan and flatleaf parsley

There is something very special about the flavour of chanterelle mushrooms. They have a heavenly apricot perfume, especially when freshly picked, and if you've been scouring the forests for these yellow beauties this recipe is as good a use for them as you'll find. If you're buying them from a shop (and I have seen them in a supermarket recently), then make sure that they are pale yellow to golden, with no brown soggy bits. They should have a firm texture and should, when sliced, be almost white inside. They're in season from late June until the end of October.

Serves 4

450 g (1 lb) chanterelle mushrooms
120 ml (4 fl oz) olive oil
75 g (3 oz) butter
225 g (8 oz) shallots, finely chopped
225 g (8 oz) arborio rice
250 ml (8 fl oz) dry white wine

900 ml (1½ pints) Chicken Stock
 (see page 181)
25 g (1 oz) Parmesan, finely grated
3 tablespoons coarsely chopped fresh flatleaf
 parsley, plus extra for garnishing
Maldon salt and freshly ground black pepper
slivers of Parmesan, to garnish

Brush any dirt off the mushrooms with a dry pastry brush and then wipe them clean with a damp cloth. Heat 2 tablespoons of the oil and 25 g (1 oz) of the butter in a large, heavy-based pan. Add the mushrooms and fry over a high heat for 2–3 minutes until they are nicely coloured. Tip them onto a plate and set aside.

Add the rest of the oil and the shallots to the pan and cook over a medium heat until the shallots are soft and lightly browned. Add the rice and stir it around for about a minute until all the grains are coated in the oil.

Add the white wine to the pan and simmer quite vigorously until it has almost disappeared. Then add 300 ml (10 fl oz) of the stock and continue to cook over a gentle heat, stirring until it has all been absorbed by the rice. Continue to cook, adding the stock 300 ml (10 fl oz) at a time, until it has all been absorbed and the rice is tender and creamy, but still with a little bit of bite left in it. This should take about 20 minutes in total.

Stir in the rest of the butter, the grated Parmesan, chopped parsley, chanterelles and salt and pepper to taste. Warm through, then remove from the heat.

Spoon the mixture into 4 warmed bowls, sprinkle with the Parmesan slivers and a little more chopped parsley, and serve with a hunk of wholemeal bread if you wish.

Whisky – the jewel in Scotland's

crown, the 'water of life' – is not just

the world's best-known spirit. For me

its complex, sometimes exotic, flavours

are an inspiration for some of my

favourite puddings.

PUDDINGS

THREE-CHOCOLATE MARQUISE

with crème fraîche sorbet

This is a bit of a restaurant dessert and requires a fair bit of time and effort, but you will be rewarded with a very sexy pudding. The crème fraîche sorbet gives just the right amount of acidity to balance the richness of the chocolate. The sorbet also works well made with mascarpone instead of crème fraîche. And it has to be said that the marquise also tastes great made with only one type of chocolate, so it then needs to be called One-Chocolate Marquise.

In the restaurant we use sheets of leaf gelatine to set this terrine but this is still not very easy to come by. Do use it instead of the powdered variety, though, if you're lucky enough to find some. You just need to soak the leaves in plenty of cold water for a few minutes, then lift them out and add them to the bowl of chocolate when you are melting it.

Serves 12

450 ml (15 fl oz) milk

8 medium farm-fresh egg yolks

75 g (3 oz) caster sugar

450 ml (15 fl oz) double cream

200 g (7 oz) milk chocolate, broken into
  small pieces

200 g (7 oz) white chocolate, broken into
  small pieces

200 g (7 oz) plain chocolate, broken into
  small pieces

4 × 11 g sachets powdered gelatine plus
  1 teaspoon, or 16 × 3 g sheets of leaf
  gelatine

For the crème fraîche sorbet:

250 g (9 oz) caster sugar

350 ml (12 fl oz) water

2 tablespoons strained fresh orange juice

500 g (1 lb 2 oz) crème fraîche

Pour the milk into a pan and bring it up to the boil. Meanwhile, cream the egg yolks with the sugar until pale and creamy. Just before the milk is about to boil over the sides of the pan, whisk it into the egg yolks. Return the mixture to the pan and cook over a gentle heat for a couple of minutes, stirring, until it lightly coats the back of a wooden spoon. Stir in the double cream, divide the mixture equally between 3 bowls and leave it to cool.

Place the milk chocolate in a heatproof bowl and bring about 2.5 cm (1 inch) of water up to a simmer in a pan. Rest the bowl of milk chocolate over the pan and leave it to melt. Add 2 sheets of the soaked leaf gelatine, if using, to the bowl. If using powdered gelatine, put 4½ tablespoons of cold water into a small pan, sprinkle over 4½ teaspoons of the gelatine and leave it to 'sponge' for 5 minutes. Melt it over a low heat until clear. Stir the dissolved gelatine and then the melted milk chocolate into one bowl of the custard and mix together well until smooth. Line a 7.5 cm (3 inch) deep, 7.5 × 25 cm (3 × 10 inch) Le Creuset or similar terrine dish with clingfilm so that it overhangs the sides and is tucked down well into the corners. Pour in the milk chocolate custard and leave it to chill in the fridge until set.

Now repeat this procedure with the white chocolate but use another 2 sheets of soaked leaf gelatine, or 5 teaspoons of powdered gelatine and 5 tablespoons of cold water. Pour this on top of the milk chocolate layer and leave it to set. Finally repeat once more using the plain chocolate, the remaining soaked leaf gelatine or 4 teaspoons of powdered gelatine and 4 tablespoons of cold water. Pour into the terrine dish and leave to set. Then cover the whole terrine with the overhanging clingfilm and leave it until you are ready to serve.

For the crème fraîche sorbet, put the sugar and water into a medium-sized pan and place over a high heat. Bring to the boil, stirring from time to time. Leave the syrup to simmer for 5 minutes, skimming off any impurities as they rise to the surface. Remove it from the heat and leave it to cool, then whisk in the orange juice and crème fraîche and chill the mixture in the fridge for a few hours until it is really cold.

Now you can either churn the mixture in an ice-cream machine or pour it into a plastic box and freeze until almost firm. If doing the latter, scrape the mixture into a food processor and whizz until smooth. Pour it back into the box and repeat one more time. Return the sorbet to the freezer and freeze until firm.

To serve, invert the marquise onto a board, cut it into 1 cm (½ inch) slices and serve with a quenelle of the crème fraîche sorbet.

Tarte Tatins

Four variations on the classic apple tarte tatin, each with its own accompaniment. Either make one big tart or little individual ones using 12.5 cm (5 inch) blini pans. These aren't as difficult as you may think, and work just fine with bought puff pastry.

BANANA TARTE TATIN

with rum cream

The love affair between the flavours of banana and rum has always been intense; they belong together, especially in a dish like this where the bananas are glossy with sticky-sweet caramelized juices and the rum is infused in cool, freshly whipped cream.

Serves 6

75 g (3 oz) caster sugar
50 g (2 oz) unsalted butter
4 large bananas
350 g (12 oz) puff pastry
flour, for rolling out pastry

For the rum cream:

1 tablespoon light muscovado sugar
2 tablespoons dark rum or to taste
300 ml (10 fl oz) double cream
a pinch of ground cinnamon, to decorate

Preheat the oven to 190°C/375°F/Gas Mark 5. If making one large tart, put the sugar and butter into a flameproof 25 cm (10 inch) cast-iron frying pan. If making smaller tarts, divide the sugar and butter evenly between six 12.5 cm (5 inch) blini pans. Cook over a medium heat, stirring now and then, until the mixture turns into a smooth toffee. It will look very grainy to start with and the butter will look as if it has split away from the sugar, but just keep stirring and it will gradually come together. Now take the pan(s) off the heat and make sure that the toffee covers the base in an even layer.

Peel the bananas and cut them sharply on the diagonal into long thick slices. Arrange them randomly over the base of the pan(s), overlapping them here and there, so that they cover the toffee in a thick layer. For the large tart, roll out the pastry on a lightly floured surface into a 28 cm (11 inch) circle – don't worry about it being too neat. For the individual tarts, divide the pastry into 6 and roll each piece out into a 15 cm (6 inch) circle. Lay the pastry over the bananas

and tuck the edges down into the pan(s) to make the rim(s) of the tart(s). Prick the top of the pastry here and there with a fork, then slide the pan(s) into the oven and bake for 25 minutes for the smaller tarts or 30 minutes for the larger one until risen and golden.

Meanwhile, make the rum cream. Mix the sugar with the rum until the sugar has dissolved. Whip the cream until it begins to show signs of thickening, then whisk in the sweetened rum until it forms soft peaks. Cover and chill until you are ready to serve.

Remove the pan(s) from the oven and leave to rest for 10 minutes. Then run a sharp knife around the pastry to make sure that all the edges are free and place an inverted plate over the top of the pan(s). Turn the two over together and remove the pan(s). Cut the large tart into 6 wedges. Serve with the rum cream, sprinkled with a little cinnamon.

PEAR AND RAISIN TARTE TATIN

with mascarpone cheese

Pears, like apples, have a lovely soft but firm texture that makes for an excellent tarte tatin. Dried raisins add little concentrated bursts of sweetness, and you can experiment by adding other dried fruits, such as apricots or dates.

Serves 6

100 g (4 oz) muscatel raisins
50 ml (2 fl oz) Muscat Beaumes de Venise or
    another sweet dessert wine
75 g (3 oz) caster sugar

50 g (2 oz) unsalted butter
900 g (2 lb) ripe but firm dessert pears
350 g (12 oz) puff pastry
flour, for rolling out pastry
200 g (7 oz) mascarpone cheese, to serve

Mix the raisins with the wine, cover and leave to soak overnight. The next day make the toffee in the pan(s) as in the recipe for *Banana Tarte Tatin* on page 132. Halve the pears, scoop out the cores with a melon baller or teaspoon and then peel. If making one large tart, arrange them over the base of the pan rounded-side down with their thin tips pointing towards the centre. For individual tarts, place 2 pear halves on the base of each pan, heel to toe so that they nestle nicely together. Fill the cavity of each one with some of the soaked raisins and scatter the rest into the gaps between each piece of fruit. Cover with the pastry, prick with a fork and bake for 25–30 minutes.

Depending on the type of pears that you have used, there might be quite a lot of syrupy juices in the bottom of the pan(s). Before you turn out the tart(s), carefully pour these off into a small pan and boil them rapidly until they become thick and toffee-like once more. Turn out the tart(s), spoon over the toffee and serve each portion with a good spoonful of mascarpone cheese.

MANGO TARTE TATIN

with crème fraîche

The crème fraîche cuts into the smooth sweetness of the mango in a most delicious way.

Serves 6

75 g (3 oz) caster sugar
50 g (2 oz) unsalted butter

1 very large or 2 smaller ripe, firm mangoes
350 g (12 oz) puff pastry
flour, for rolling out pastry
200 ml (7 fl oz) crème fraîche, to serve

Make the tart(s) in the same way as the *Banana Tarte Tatin* on page 132, using the mangoes instead of the bananas. Peel the mangoes and slice the fruit away from either side of the thin flat stone in 2 whole pieces. Place the slices of fruit cut-side down on a board and slice into long 1 cm (½ inch) thick slices. Then cut away any bits of fruit left on the stone and use them to fill in any gaps. Assemble and bake the tart(s) as before and serve with scoops of crème fraîche instead of the rum cream.

FRESH FIG TARTE TATIN

with fromage blanc

There's something luxurious about fresh figs – I think it's the rich, red-purple colour of the flesh. The golden, crisp pastry combined with the soft acidity of fromage blanc makes this a real star dish.

Serves 6

75 g (3 oz) caster sugar
50 g (2 oz) unsalted butter

8 ripe figs, halved
350 g (12 oz) puff pastry
Flour, for rolling out pastry
200 ml (7 fl oz) fromage blanc, to serve

Make the tart(s) in the same way as the *Banana Tarte Tatin* on page 132, using the figs instead of the bananas. Serve with fromage blanc (or fromage frais) instead of rum cream.

HOT PASSION FRUIT SOUFFLÉS

I like to make these little soufflés using 3–4 passion fruit for each one so that you get a really sherbety taste, but you could cut the number of fruit by half and make the 'jam' with just 25 g (1 oz) caster sugar if you wish. The usual soufflé rules apply here but for some reason these seem to rise higher than any other soufflé I know.

Serves 6

24 passion fruit
190 g (6½ oz) caster sugar, plus extra for
   dusting and to serve
a little butter for greasing

350 ml (12 fl oz) milk
3 medium farm-fresh egg yolks
15 g (½ oz) cornflour
15 g (½ oz) plain flour
6 medium farm-fresh egg whites

Cut each passion fruit in half and scoop out the pulp into a small pan. Add 50 g (2 oz) of the sugar and stir over a gentle heat until the sugar has dissolved. Bring the mixture to the boil and boil it rapidly for about 10 minutes, stirring frequently towards the end of the cooking, until you are left with a thick 'jam'. Pass this through a sieve to remove the seeds and set aside.

Slide a baking sheet onto the middle shelf of the oven and preheat it to 200°C/400°F/ Gas Mark 6. Lightly butter six 7.5 cm (3 inch) ramekins and dust them out with a little extra caster sugar.

Pour all but 1 tablespoon of the milk into a pan and slowly bring it to the boil. Meanwhile, beat the egg yolks, another 40 g (1½ oz) caster sugar, the cornflour, plain flour and remaining milk together in a bowl until smooth. Whisk in the hot milk, return the mixture to the pan and bring to the boil, stirring. Reduce the heat and leave the mixture to simmer very gently for about 10 minutes, beating it every now and then, until you have cooked out the taste of the flour.

Pour the custard into a bowl and beat in the passion fruit jam. Whisk the egg whites into soft peaks and then whisk in the remaining caster sugar. Lightly whisk one-quarter of the whites into the custard to loosen it slightly, then carefully fold in the remainder. Spoon the mixture into the prepared ramekins, level the tops and then run the tip of a knife around the inside edge of each dish to release the mixture. Slide the ramekins onto the baking sheet and bake for 10–12 minutes until the soufflés are well risen, browned and doubled in height but still slightly wobbly. Quickly lift them onto small dessert plates, sprinkle with a little more caster (or icing) sugar and serve straight away before they've got time to sink.

TUILE OF LEMON CURD ICE-CREAM

with strawberry sauce

Instead of making the ice-cream, you could stir some good-quality lemon curd into some good vanilla ice-cream and freeze it once more until firm. For the strawberry sauce, you need to check out the sweetness of your strawberries and add only enough sugar to taste. The tuiles make great little nests to hold the ice-cream and sauce.

Serves 6

For the lemon curd:
2 farm-fresh eggs
finely grated zest and juice of 1 large lemon
75 g (3 oz) caster sugar
50 g (2 oz) unsalted butter

For the ice-cream:
600 ml (1 pint) milk
6 medium farm-fresh egg yolks
75 g (3 oz) caster sugar
225 ml (8 fl oz) double cream

For the tuile baskets:
25 g (1 oz) caster sugar
25 g (1 oz) plain flour
1 medium farm-fresh egg white
25 g (1 oz) melted butter

For the strawberry sauce:
350 g (12 oz) fresh strawberries, hulled
75 g (3 oz) caster sugar or to taste

For the lemon curd, beat the eggs together and then strain them through a sieve into a heatproof bowl. Add the lemon zest and juice, sugar and butter and rest the bowl over a pan of barely simmering water. Cook, stirring, for about 20 minutes until the mixture is smooth and thickened. Remove the bowl from the pan and leave the curd to cool.

For the ice-cream, pour the milk into a pan and slowly bring to the boil. Meanwhile, whisk the egg yolks and sugar together until pale and creamy. Whisk in the hot milk, return the mixture to the pan and cook over a gentle heat, stirring continuously, until it lightly coats the back of a wooden spoon. Pour into a bowl, leave to cool and then stir in the double cream. Cover and leave in the fridge until the mixture is really cold and then stir in the lemon curd. Now you can either churn the mixture in an ice-cream machine or pour it into a plastic box and freeze until almost firm. If you are doing the latter, scrape the mixture into a food processor and whizz until smooth. Pour it back into the box and repeat the process once more. Return the ice-cream to the freezer and freeze until firm.

For the tuile baskets, put the sugar, flour and egg white into a bowl and beat together into a smooth paste. Beat in the melted butter and leave the mixture to chill in the fridge for 20 minutes. Preheat the oven to 180°C/350°F/Gas Mark 4. Then drop about 3 teaspoons of the mixture well apart onto a lightly greased baking tray and spread it out very thinly into approximately 13 cm (5 inch) circles. Bake for 6–8 minutes until golden brown around the edges. Remove from the oven, leave to cool for a few seconds and then quickly lift off the baking sheet with a palette knife and drape over the bottom of 3 upturned ramekins or small pudding moulds. Pleat the biscuits into a cup-shape and leave to cool and go crisp. Repeat with the rest of the mixture.

For the strawberry sauce, slice the strawberries into a bowl, stir in the sugar and leave for a few minutes until they have become juicy. Whizz the mixture in a liquidizer or with a hand blender until smooth and then press through a sieve into a clean bowl. Cover and chill.

To serve, scoop the ice-cream into neat balls and drop them into the tuile baskets. Place the baskets on dessert plates and spoon some of the strawberry sauce around them.

CLOOTIE DUMPLING

with clotted cream

A real Scottish dish and none the worse for that, traditionally made in an old pillowcase. I recently judged a clootie dumpling competition and I learned that a perfect pudding should be as spherical as possible, have an unblemished shiny coating and a dense, moist, flavoursome interior. Clotted cream is the perfect accompaniment.

Serves 8

225 g (8 oz) plain flour, plus 25 g (1 oz) for sprinkling
1 teaspoon bicarbonate of soda
1 teaspoon mixed spice
1 teaspoon ground cinnamon
1 teaspoon ground ginger
¼ teaspoon Maldon salt
175 g (6 oz) caster sugar, plus 1 tablespoon for sprinkling

100 g (4 oz) shredded suet
100 g (4 oz) sultanas
75 g (3 oz) currants
75 g (3 oz) chopped, stoned dates
50 g (2 oz) muscatel raisins
1 apple or carrot, coarsely grated
1 tablespoon black treacle
1 medium farm-fresh egg
150 ml (5 fl oz) buttermilk
225 g (8 oz) clotted cream, to serve

Sift the flour, bicarbonate of soda, spices and salt into a bowl and stir in the sugar, suet, dried fruits and the grated apple or carrot. Mix the black treacle with the egg and some of the buttermilk and mix into the dry ingredients to give a soft mixture with a cake-like dropping consistency.

Dip a large piece of muslin, an old pillowcase, a pudding cloth or a tea towel into boiling water, remove it and squeeze out the excess water. Lay it out on a surface and sprinkle a 30 cm (12 inch) circle in the centre with the 25 g (1 oz) of flour and the tablespoon of caster sugar. Spoon the pudding mixture on top and then bring the opposite corners of the cloth together over the top and tie securely with string, leaving a little room for the pudding to expand.

Rest a large heatproof plate in the base of a large pan on some sort of trivet or container so that it is not in direct contact with the heat and place the pudding on the plate, knotted side up. Pour in enough water almost to cover the pudding, cover with a tight-fitting lid and simmer gently for 3¾–4 hours. Take a peek every now and then to check the water level and top it up if necessary.

Preheat the oven to 180°C/350°F/Gas Mark 4. Lift the pudding out of the pan and dip it briefly in a bowl of cold water – this will ensure that the outside of the pudding does not stick to the cloth when you unwrap it. Undo the parcel, fold back the cloth and invert the pudding onto an ovenproof serving plate. Slide it into the oven and leave it for about 15 minutes until the outside of the pudding has dried off. Serve in chunky wedges with scoops of clotted cream and perhaps a small glass of whisky.

FROZEN CHOCOLATE CAKE

with mascarpone

One from my pal Jim Kerr (chef, not singer) who is now the general manager of my new Glasgow restaurant, Nairns. This chocolate cake is very nice and a little goes a long way. The mascarpone helps it slip down a treat. (Note that the mascarpone has raw egg yolk in it, in case that's a problem for you.)

Serves 8

200 g (7 oz) bitter plain chocolate (65 per
   cent cocoa solids)
200 g (7 oz) caster sugar
200 g (7 oz) unsalted butter
150 ml (5 fl oz) espresso coffee
3 medium farm-fresh eggs

For the mascarpone:
250 g (9 oz) mascarpone cheese
1 tablespoon caster sugar
1 medium farm-fresh egg yolk

For the frozen chocolate cake, line a 20 × 30 cm (8 × 12 inch) shallow rectangular tin with non-stick baking parchment. Preheat the oven to 180°C/350°F/Gas Mark 4.

Break the chocolate into a pan and add the sugar, butter and espresso coffee. Leave it over a low heat until everything has melted and then increase the heat slightly and allow the mixture to come up to a gentle simmer. Leave it to simmer for 10 minutes, stirring frequently, until the mixture has slightly caramelized.

Break the eggs into a bowl and whisk together lightly. Beat in the caramelized chocolate mixture and mix together well. Pour the mixture through a sieve into the prepared tin and bake in the centre of the oven for 30 minutes. Remove the cake from the oven and leave it to cool. Then transfer it to the freezer and leave it until it has just frozen, but not so that it is rock hard.

Meanwhile, beat the mascarpone together with the caster sugar and egg yolk in a bowl until thick. Cover with clingfilm and chill in the fridge.

To serve, remove the cake from the freezer and lift it out of the tin. Peel back the baking parchment and cut the cake in half lengthways and then across into 4 so that you end up with 8 rectangular pieces. Lift onto dessert plates and serve with quenelles of the mascarpone.

OATY RHUBARB CRUMBLES

with rhubarb sauce and crème anglaise

Crumbles have long been a favourite of mine but they do not make very attractive restaurant-style puddings. However, layering up the components in large metal pastry rings solves the problem and the two different sauces make them look stunning.

Serves 6

900 g (2 lb) rhubarb, trimmed
6 slices fresh root ginger
pared zest of 1 small orange
175 g (6 oz) caster sugar

For the crumble mixture:
275 g (10 oz) plain flour

150 g (5 oz) butter
100 g (4 oz) soft light brown sugar
75 g (3 oz) rolled oats

For the crème anglaise:
½ vanilla pod
300 ml (10 fl oz) milk
3 medium farm-fresh egg yolks
25 g (1 oz) caster sugar

For the crème anglaise, split open the vanilla pod and scrape out all the little black seeds. Put the pod and the seeds into a small pan with the milk and bring to the boil. Remove from the heat and leave to infuse for 20 minutes.

Preheat the oven to 200°C/400°F/Gas Mark 6. Cut the rhubarb into 2.5 cm (1 inch) pieces and place in a pan with the sliced ginger, orange zest and sugar. Cover and cook over a gentle heat for a few minutes, stirring very gently every now and then, until the rhubarb is only just tender and still holding its shape. Tip the mixture into a sieve set over a small clean pan, discard the pieces of ginger and orange zest and set the rhubarb aside to allow the syrup to drain out of it.

Meanwhile, sift the flour into a large bowl and rub in the butter until the mixture looks like fine breadcrumbs. Stir in 2 tablespoons of the sugar. Place six 10 cm (4 inch) lightly buttered metal pastry cutters on a baking sheet and spoon about 2 tablespoons of the flour and butter mixture into the base of each one. Spread out evenly and then press down very lightly with the back of the spoon. Stir the rest of the sugar and the rolled oats into the remaining crumble mixture.

Divide the rhubarb between each ring, level the tops and then cover with a layer of the crumble topping. Bake for 25–30 minutes until crisp and golden. Meanwhile, finish the crème anglaise. Beat the egg yolks and caster sugar together in a bowl until pale and creamy. Bring the milk back to the boil, lift out the vanilla pod and whisk the hot milk into the egg yolks. Return the mixture to the pan and cook over a gentle heat, stirring continuously, until it lightly coats the back of a wooden spoon. Keep the crème anglaise warm. Gently warm the rhubarb syrup.

To serve, slide a fish slice under each crumble and place in the centre of a warmed dessert plate. Carefully lift off the cutters and pour around some of the rhubarb sauce and crème anglaise.

WALNUT AND WHISKY TARTS

with athol brose cream

These are a bit like mini pecan pies but made with walnuts and flavoured with Scotch whisky instead of the more classic bourbon. They are definitely for those of you with a sweet tooth, but serve them with plain whipped cream to cut through some of this richness if you prefer.

Serves 6

65 g (2½ oz) butter
75 g (3 oz) light muscovado sugar
2 medium farm-fresh eggs
175 ml (6 fl oz) golden syrup
1½ tablespoons whisky
a pinch of salt
115 g (4½ oz) walnut pieces
1½ tablespoons plain flour

6 x 10 cm (4 inch) Sweet Pastry *tartlet cases*
  (see page 188)
100 g (4 oz) walnut halves, to decorate

For the athol brose cream:
150 ml (5 fl oz) double cream
1½ tablespoons clear honey
  (heather if possible)
50 ml (2 fl oz) whisky

Preheat the oven to 180°C/350°F/Gas Mark 4. Beat the butter and muscovado sugar together until pale and fluffy. Beat in the eggs, one at a time, and then slowly mix in the golden syrup, whisky and salt. Mix the walnut pieces with the flour and fold them into the egg mixture. Pour into the sweet pastry cases and bake in the oven for 10 minutes until the filling is lightly set and has formed a thin crust over the surface.

Remove the tartlets from the oven and lower the temperature to 160°C/325°F/Gas Mark 3. Arrange a ring of walnut halves around the outside edge of each tart, return them to the oven and bake for another 10 minutes until completely set.

Meanwhile, for the athol brose cream, whisk the cream until it begins to thicken. Slowly whisk in the honey and then the whisky until the mixture forms soft peaks.

Remove the tartlets from the oven and leave them to cool a little until warm. Then carefully lift them out of the tins onto dessert plates and serve with some of the athol brose cream.

DRAMBUIE AND PRUNE CUSTARD TART

Most people associate prunes with armagnac, probably because they come from the same area of south-west France. However, they also conjoin sublimely with Drambuie, especially the Agen prunes, which are plump, sweet and flavoursome. Drambuie is not only my favourite post-prandial tipple, but the liqueur that I use most often in my cooking. There's just something in that combination of honey, spices and whisky that brings out or accentuates other flavours. The whisky with the history and the mystery! Mine's a large one, thank you!

Serves 8

350 g (12 oz) dried Agen or other
  good-quality prunes
75 ml (3 fl oz) Drambuie
1 tablespoon soft light brown sugar
300 ml (10 fl oz) double cream
150 ml (5 fl oz) milk

4 medium farm-fresh eggs
50 g (2 oz) caster sugar
1 teaspoon vanilla extract
1 tablespoon plain flour
1 × 25 cm (10 inch) Sweet Pastry tart case
  (see page 188)
icing sugar, to decorate
pouring cream (optional), to serve

Make a slit in the side of each prune and hook out the stones with the tip of a knife. Reshape the fruit and put them into a bowl with the Drambuie and brown sugar. Cover and leave to soak overnight. The next day, slide a baking sheet into the oven and preheat it to 180°C/350°C/Gas Mark 4.

Drain the prunes, reserving any juices. Put the cream and milk into a pan and slowly bring just up to the boil. Meanwhile, whisk the eggs, caster sugar, vanilla and flour until well combined. Whisk in the hot cream and milk and any Drambuie juices left over from the prunes.

Arrange the prunes over the base of the pastry case. Pull out the oven shelf with the baking sheet, slide on the tart tin and then pour over the custard mixture. Carefully slide the shelf back into the oven and bake the tart for 30–35 minutes until just set. Remove from the oven and leave to cool. Sprinkle the edges of the tart with a little icing sugar and serve cut into wedges, with a little extra pouring cream if you like.

LITTLE SCOTTISH BUTTERSCOTCH POTS

with Viennese shortbread fingers

These little puds are like a cross between a crème brûlée (without the top) and a mousse. What makes them so special is the 'toffee', which you make by boiling a can of sweetened condensed milk until it caramelizes inside the tin. All they then need is a thin layer of unwhipped cream flooded over the top. If you like, you can use the biscuits to scoop out the mixture. Yum!

Serves 6

1 x 200 g (7 oz) can sweetened
    condensed milk
6 medium farm-fresh egg yolks
375 ml (13 fl oz) double cream, plus extra
    to serve

For the Viennese shortbread fingers
    (makes 12):

75 g (3 oz) butter, slightly softened
25 g (1 oz) icing sugar, plus extra for dusting
25 g (1 oz) cornflour
50 g (2 oz) plain flour

Place the unopened can of condensed milk in a pan and cover it with cold water. Bring to the boil and leave to simmer for 3 hours, topping up the water every now and then so that it always covers the can. Leave to cool in the water.

Preheat the oven to 150°C/300°F/Gas Mark 2. Open the can of 'toffee' and scrape it into a bowl. Stir in the egg yolks and then gradually stir in the double cream until you have a smooth mixture. Strain it into a jug and then pour it evenly into six 7.5 cm (3 inch) ramekins. Place them in a small roasting tin and pour in boiling water until it comes half-way up the sides of the dishes. Slide the roasting tin onto the middle shelf of the oven and cook for 20–25 minutes until just set but still a little wobbly. Remove the ramekins from the roasting tin, leave to cool and then cover and chill for at least a couple of hours.

For the biscuits, increase the oven temperature to 180°C/350°F/Gas Mark 4. Lightly grease and flour a baking tray. Beat the butter with the sugar until pale and creamy. Sift the cornflour and flour together and then beat into the butter mixture until smooth. Spoon the mixture into a piping bag fitted with a large star nozzle and pipe twelve 7.5 cm (3 inch) fingers spaced well apart onto the prepared baking sheet. Chill in the fridge for 30 minutes. Bake the biscuits for 10–12 minutes until golden. Leave to go cold and then carefully lift them off the baking sheet.

To serve, pour a thin layer of unwhipped cream onto the top of each butterscotch pot. Dust the shortbread fingers with a little icing sugar and serve alongside the pots.

AMARETTI AND PEACH TRIFLE

with mascarpone cream

There are a lot of trifle variations doing the rounds at the moment and this Italian-inspired version is my effort. Use top-quality white peaches if you can, but there are some pretty good tinned ones around, although they are generally more expensive than the fresh ones. I like to serve a glass of chilled Italian dessert wine with this trifle. Please note, in case it's a problem for you, that this recipe has raw eggs in it.

Serves 6

150 g (5 oz) amaretti biscuits
3 tablespoons Kirsch or amontillado sherry
6 large, juicy fresh peaches

275 g (10 oz) mascarpone
2 medium farm-fresh eggs, separated
50 g (2 oz) caster sugar
150 ml (5 fl oz) double cream
75 g (3 oz) granulated sugar

Place the amaretti biscuits in a deep, glass serving dish and sprinkle over the Kirsch or sherry. Set aside, turning the biscuits over every now and then, until they have soaked up all the liquid. Meanwhile, place the peaches in a large bowl and cover with boiling water. Leave for 30 seconds and then drain and cover with cold water. Peel off the skins, halve to remove the stones and then cut the peaches into slices directly over the trifle bowl so that you don't lose any of the juices. Spread the fruit out into an even layer.

Beat the mascarpone and egg yolks together in a bowl until smooth and creamy. Beat in the sugar. Whisk the double cream until it just begins to thicken and then gently stir it into the mascarpone. Whisk the egg whites into soft peaks and lightly fold them into the mascarpone cream. The finished mixture should be quite soft and light. Spoon the mixture over the top of the peaches. Lightly level the top and chill in the refrigerator for 3–4 hours.

Now put the granulated sugar into a heavy-based pan and cook over a medium–high heat until it has melted and turned into liquid caramel. Meanwhile, mark a circle about 2.5 cm (1 inch) smaller than the diameter of your trifle dish on a piece of non-stick baking parchment. Remove the caramel from the heat and drizzle it back and forth over the paper using a spoon, taking care not to go outside the edge of the circle. What you want to do is create a sort of caramel cobweb. Leave it to cool and go hard and then carefully lift it off the paper and lower it on top of the trifle just before serving.

CHAMPAGNE JELLIES

with a citrus fruit salad

These lovely translucent jellies look stunning with the multicoloured citrus pieces floating in their passion fruit sea. I'm getting a bit carried away with the prose, but this is a refreshing and stylish way to end a meal.

Serves 4

350 ml (12 fl oz) champagne or sparkling dry
   white wine
250 g (9 oz) caster sugar
1 × 11 g sachet powdered gelatine or
   4 × 3 g sheets leaf of gelatine

For the citrus fruit salad:

12 passion fruit
caster sugar, to taste
2 ruby grapefruit
2 oranges
1 lemon
1 lime

For the jellies, put the champagne or sparkling wine and sugar into a pan and leave over a gentle heat until the sugar has dissolved. Meanwhile, if using leaf gelatine, leave it to soak in cold water for a few minutes and then lift it out, stir it into the champagne mixture and leave until dissolved. If using powdered gelatine, put 3 tablespoons of cold water into a small pan, sprinkle over the powder and leave it to 'sponge' for 5 minutes. Heat very gently until clear and then stir into the champagne mixture. Pour into 4 wet dariole or mini-pudding moulds and leave to set in the fridge overnight.

The next day, make the citrus fruit salad. Halve the passion fruit and scoop out the pulp into a sieve. Set over a small pan. Press out the juice with a wooden spoon and reserve a few of the seeds for decoration. Discard the rest. Cook the juice over a gentle heat until it thickens, then stir in a little caster sugar to taste. Leave to go cold and chill until needed.

Slice the top and bottom off each citrus fruit and then cut away all the skin and white pith with a small, sharp knife. Cut either side of each dividing membrane to remove the fruit in neat segments and then stir them into the passion fruit juice.

To serve, dip the moulds very briefly in warm water and turn the jellies out into the centres of 4 dessert plates. Spoon the citrus fruit salad around them and sprinkle with the reserved passion fruit seeds.

Crème Brûlées

I'm pretty sure I'm on record as having stated that vanilla is the only flavouring that should be used in crème brûlée. However, a period of experimentation has caused me to change my mind on that one, and I offer you four alternatives. The secret of making brûlées that set in the fridge is (1) to whisk the egg yolks over simmering water until a strand from the whisk will lie on the surface of the mixture, and (2) to ensure that the cream is just about to boil over before pouring it onto the yolks. That way the mix cooks out in seconds rather than the more usual quarter of an hour of stirring. Always use a wooden spoon to stir the mix once it is back in the pan and use a side-to-side motion rather than a circular one. This moves the milk about more and prevents that scrambled egg thing happening in the bottom of the pan.

EGG NOG CRÈME BRÛLÉE

Here, advocaat brings out the egginess in the brûlée mixture, but it still needs the vanilla to make it sing.

Serves 6

600 ml (1 pint) double cream
6 medium farm-fresh egg yolks
50 g (2 oz) caster sugar

For the flavouring and topping:

1 vanilla pod
6 tablespoons advocaat liqueur
½ teaspoon freshly grated nutmeg
6 heaped teaspoons demerara sugar

Split open the vanilla pod and scrape out the seeds into a pan. Add the cream and the pod and slowly bring up to the boil. Put the egg yolks and caster sugar into a bowl and rest over a pan on simmering water. Whisk until the mixture is very pale and thick.

Just before the cream boils over the sides of the pan, pour two-thirds onto the egg yolks and whisk together. Pour the mixture back into the pan containing the remaining cream and stir over a low heat for 2–3 minutes until it is thick and coats the back of a spoon. Remove the pan from the heat and stir for another couple of minutes. Remove the vanilla pod and stir in the advocaat and the nutmeg. Pour the mixture into six 7.5 cm (3 inch) ramekins, taking the mixture right to the top. Leave them to set in the fridge for at least 6 hours and preferably overnight.

To serve, preheat the grill to its highest setting (or you can use a blowtorch). Sprinkle the tops of the brûlées with the demerara sugar, making sure you take it right to the edges of the ramekins, and slide them under the grill for 2–3 minutes until the sugar has caramelized. Remove and leave until the sugar toppings have cooled and gone hard before serving.

ESPRESSO COFFEE BRÛLÉE

You need top-quality coffee beans for the right flavour here. Espresso has that lovely, slightly bitter edge. Otherwise, cheat and use 2 teaspoons instant espresso coffee granules.

Serves 6

600 ml (1 pint) double cream
6 medium farm-fresh egg yolks
50 g (2 oz) caster sugar

For the flavouring and topping:
1½ tablespoons ground espresso coffee beans
3 tablespoons coffee liqueur, such as
   Tía Maria
6 heaped teaspoons soft light brown sugar

Put the ground coffee and the cream into a pan and slowly bring up to the boil. Put the egg yolks and caster sugar into a bowl and rest over a pan of simmering water. Whisk until the mixture is very pale and thick.

Just before the cream boils over the sides of the pan, pour two-thirds onto the egg yolks through a muslin-lined sieve and whisk together. Pour the mixture back into the pan containing the remaining cream and stir over a low heat for 2–3 minutes until it is thick and coats the back of a spoon. Remove the pan from the heat and stir for another couple of minutes. Stir in the coffee liqueur and pour the mixture into six 7.5 cm (3 inch) ramekins, taking the mixture right to the top. Leave them to set in the fridge for at least 6 hours and preferably overnight.

To serve, preheat the grill to its highest setting (or you can use a blowtorch). Sprinkle the top of the brûlées with the soft brown sugar, making sure you take it right to the edges of the ramekins, and slide them under the grill for 2–3 minutes until the sugar has caramelized. Remove and leave until the sugar topping has cooled and gone hard before serving.

ORANGE CRÈME BRÛLÉE

Drambuie again, this time with one of its favourite partners, oranges. Use small, sweet, seedless oranges for this.

Serves 6

2–3 small, thin-skinned oranges
6 tablespoons Drambuie liqueur
finely grated zest (or pared zest) of
  ½ small orange

2–4 whole cloves
600 ml (1 pint) double cream
6 medium farm-fresh egg yolks
50 g (2 oz) caster sugar, plus 6 heaped
  teaspoons for sprinkling

Slice the top and the bottom off each orange and sit each one on a board. Slice away the outer skin so that there is no white pith left behind and then slice each orange across into thin slices. Place about 3 slices in the bottom of each 7.5 cm (3 inch) ramekin and spoon over 1 tablespoon of the Drambuie.

Put the orange zest, the cloves and the cream into a pan and slowly bring up to the boil. Put the egg yolks and caster sugar into a bowl and rest over a pan on simmering water. Whisk until the mixture is very pale and thick.

Just before the cream boils over the sides of the pan, pour two-thirds onto the egg yolks and whisk together. Pour the mixture back into the pan containing the remaining cream and stir over a low heat for 2–3 minutes until it is thick and coats the back of a spoon. Remove the pan from the heat and stir for another couple of minutes. Pour the mixture through a muslin-lined sieve into the ramekins, taking the mixture right to the top. Leave them to set in the fridge for at least 6 hours and preferably overnight.

To serve, preheat the grill to its highest setting (or you can use a blowtorch). Sprinkle the top of the brûlées with the caster sugar, making sure you take it right to the edges of the ramekins, and slide them under the grill for 2–3 minutes until the sugar has caramelized. Remove and leave until the sugar topping has cooled and gone hard before serving.

SUMMER BERRY BRÛLÉE

The great thing about this is the lovely puddle of fruity caramel juices at the bottom of the pot, which soak into the custard.

Serves 6

75 g (3 oz) granulated sugar, plus 6 heaped teaspoons
175 g (6 oz) mixed prepared blueberries, blackcurrants and redcurrants
175 g (6 oz) raspberries and halved small strawberries
1 vanilla pod
600 ml (1 pint) double cream
6 medium farm-fresh egg yolks
50 g (2 oz) caster sugar

Put the 75 g (3 oz) of granulated sugar into a heavy-based pan and cook over a medium heat until it dissolves and cooks to a light brown caramel. Take the pan off the heat and stir in the blueberries, blackcurrants and redcurrants. The heat of the caramel will cook these fruits a little but the caramel will start to harden around them so return it to a low heat and warm it gently until it has dissolved. Stir in the raspberries and strawberries and divide the mixture between six 7.5 cm (3 inch) ramekins.

Split open the vanilla pod and scrape out the seeds into a pan. Add the cream and the pod and slowly bring up to the boil. Put the egg yolks and caster sugar into a bowl and rest over a pan on simmering water. Whisk until the mixture is very pale and thick.

Just before the cream boils over the sides of the pan, pour two-thirds onto the egg yolks and whisk together. Pour the mixture back into the pan containing the remaining cream and stir over a low heat for 2–3 minutes until it is thick and coats the back of a spoon. Remove the pan from the heat and stir for another couple of minutes. Remove the vanilla pod and pour the mixture into the ramekins, taking the mixture right to the top. Leave them to set in the fridge for at least 6 hours and preferably overnight.

To serve, preheat the grill to its highest setting (or you can use a blowtorch). Sprinkle the top of the brûlées with the remaining granulated sugar, making sure you take it right to the edges of the ramekins, and slide them under the grill for 2–3 minutes until the sugar has caramelized. Remove and leave until the sugar topping has cooled and gone hard before serving.

BLOOD ORANGE TRICKLE TART

with a compote of oranges and caramel chip ice-cream

Blood oranges are worth finding when they are in season as they not only have a fabulous colour, but also a more intense flavour than their more ordinary relatives. The crunchy caramel ice-cream gives the killer blow here. Warm tart streaked with syrup, orange salad and crunchy caramel ice-cream. Who could ask for more!

Serves 8-12

100 g (4 oz) butter, softened

175 g (6 oz) caster sugar

finely grated zest of 1 large orange

2 medium farm-fresh eggs

175 g (6 oz) self-raising flour

*5 tablespoons freshly squeezed blood
    orange juice*

*1 × 25 cm (10 inch) Sweet Pastry tart case
    (see page 188)*

100 g (4 oz) granulated sugar

For the caramel chip ice-cream:

1 vanilla pod

600 ml (1 pint) milk

6 medium farm-fresh egg yolks

75 g (3 oz) caster sugar

300 ml (10 fl oz) double cream

100 g (4 oz) granulated sugar

For the compote of oranges:

3 blood oranges

3 small, thin-skinned ordinary oranges

2 tablespoons caster sugar or to taste

First make the ice-cream so that it has plenty of time to freeze. Split open the vanilla pod and scrape out the seeds into a pan. Add the milk and the vanilla pod and bring to the boil. Set aside for 20 minutes to allow the vanilla to flavour the milk. Then bring the milk back to the boil. Meanwhile, beat the egg yolks and sugar together in a bowl until pale and creamy. Remove the vanilla pod from the milk and whisk the hot milk into the egg yolks. Return the mixture to the pan and cook over a gentle heat, stirring continuously, until the mixture lightly coats the back of a wooden spoon. Pour into a bowl and leave to cool. Stir in the double cream and leave it to chill in the fridge for 1 hour. Now you can either churn the mixture in an ice-cream maker or pour it into a shallow plastic box and leave it in the freezer until almost firm. If you do the latter, scrape the mixture into a food processor and whizz it until smooth – this will break down all the ice crystals in the mixture. Scrape the mixture back into the box, return to the freezer and leave once more until almost firm.

While the ice-cream is either churning in the machine or just before you are ready to whizz the hand-made ice-cream for the last time, put the granulated sugar into a heavy-based pan and leave over a medium–high heat until it dissolves and cooks to a golden brown caramel. Pour onto a non-stick baking sheet and leave to cool and go hard. Whizz the ice-cream for the last time. Break the caramel into little pieces and stir them into the ice-cream. Return the ice-cream to the freezer until very firm or until required. If you make your ice-cream some time in advance, remove from the freezer to the fridge about 30 minutes before you want to serve it to allow it to soften slightly.

For the tart, preheat the oven to 180°C/350°F/Gas Mark 4. To make the filling, cream the butter, sugar and orange zest together in a bowl until very pale and thick. Beat the eggs into the creamed mixture one at a time, adding 1 spoonful of the flour with the second egg. Sift over the rest of the flour and gently fold in with 1 tablespoon of the orange juice to give the mixture a dropping consistency. Spread it into the base of the sweet pastry case and bake in the oven for 30 minutes until golden brown.

Meanwhile, strain the rest of the blood orange juice into a bowl and stir in the granulated sugar. Also prepare the compote of oranges. Slice the tops and bottoms off the oranges and then cut away all the skin and white pith with a small, sharp knife. Cut either side of each dividing membrane to remove the fruit in neat segments and mix them together in a bowl with the sugar. As soon as the tart is ready, remove it from the oven and quickly spoon over the blood orange syrup mixture, leaving some of the sponge filling untouched. This will give the tart an almost stripy look when you cut into it. Leave it for a few minutes to cool slightly and allow the syrup to soak into the sponge.

Remove the tart from the tin and cut it into wedges. Place one piece on each plate and spoon some of the orange compote alongside. Add a scoop of the caramel chip ice-cream and serve the tart while it is still warm.

WARM BUTTER CAKE

with plums poached in kir

This butter cake is very rich and very moreish. It can be cooked a couple of days ahead and kept in an airtight tin if you wish. The plums improve with keeping, making this an easy pudding for a dinner party. Just warm the cake in a low oven for 10 minutes and heat the plums gently in a saucepan, but don't let them boil. Be warned, there will be requests for second helpings.

Serves 8

6 medium farm-fresh egg yolks
250 g (9 oz) plain flour
190 g (6½ oz) caster sugar
225 g (8 oz) butter, at room temperature and
    cut into small pieces, plus extra for greasing

For the plums:

900 g (2 lb) (about 24) red-skinned or
    Victoria plums
175 g (6 oz) caster sugar
300 ml (10 fl oz) white wine
2 tablespoons crème de cassis liqueur (kir)

Preheat the oven to 190°C/375°F/Gas Mark 5. Grease a 4 cm (1½ inch) deep, 25 cm (10 inch) flan tin with plenty of butter. Lightly beat the egg yolks together in a small bowl. Sift the flour into a bowl and make a dip in the middle. Add almost all the egg yolks (leaving about 1 tablespoon for glazing the tart at the end), the sugar and the butter and gradually mix the ingredients together until you have a smooth dough. Transfer the dough to the prepared tin and press it out evenly using lightly floured hands, making sure that the top is smooth. Brush the cake with the reserved egg yolk and then mark with a squiggly criss-cross pattern using the back of a fork. Bake the cake for 15 minutes and then lower the oven temperature to 160°C/325°F/Gas Mark 3 and bake for a further 15 minutes until the top is golden.

While the cake is baking, halve the plums and remove the stones. Put the sugar and wine into a large pan and bring to the boil. Add the crème de cassis and the prepared plums and leave to simmer very gently for 1–2 minutes until just tender (this will depend on the ripeness of your plums). Lift the plums out of the syrup with a slotted spoon and transfer to a shallow dish. Boil the remaining syrup for 5–6 minutes until it has reduced to a coating consistency. Leave it to cool a little and then pour it back over the plums. This is quite important because if the syrup is too hot it will continue to cook the plums even more, which you don't want. They must be served warm, too, not hot.

Remove the butter cake from the oven, leave it to cool in the tin for 15 minutes and then turn it out onto a wire rack. Serve the cake warm, cut into wedges, with the poached plums.

STEM GINGER AND BLACK TREACLE PUDDINGS

with ginger toffee sauce

A type of sponge that doesn't have to be steamed, these puddings have a lovely dense, moist texture with the flavour of ginger permeating every mouthful.

Serves 4

175 g (6 oz) stem ginger
2 tablespoons stem ginger syrup
75 g (3 oz) plain flour
¼ teaspoon ground ginger
¼ teaspoon baking powder
¼ rounded teaspoon bicarbonate of soda
1 medium farm-fresh egg

45 g (1½ oz) butter, softened
50 g (2 oz) dark muscovado sugar
1 tablespoon black treacle

For the ginger toffee sauce:
50 g (2 oz) dark muscovado sugar
50 g (2 oz) butter
150 ml (5 fl oz) double cream

Slide a baking tray onto the middle shelf of the oven and preheat it to 180°C/350°F/GasMark 4. Lightly grease four 100 ml (4 fl oz) non-stick pudding moulds with a little butter.

Put the stem ginger and the syrup into a food processor and give it a whizz until the ginger is finely chopped but not completely smooth. Spoon half of it into a small pan and add the sauce ingredients to it. Set aside.

Sift the flour, ground ginger, baking powder and bicarbonate of soda into a bowl. Add the egg, softened butter, sugar and black treacle and beat together until smooth. Beat in 75 ml (3 fl oz) of warm water and the remaining whizzed ginger.

Spoon the mixture into the prepared moulds and bake in the oven for 20–25 minutes. Meanwhile, stir the sauce ingredients together over a low heat until heated through and smooth. Turn out the puddings onto dessert plates and spoon over the ginger toffee sauce. Serve immediately.

CROWDIE

with muscat-soaked raisins and oatmeal biscuits

A pudding for those odd people who don't have a sweet tooth. It's based loosely on a classic French dessert called coeur à la crème, made with a curd-like cheese. I prefer it made with crowdie, which is Scottish cheese curds; ricotta is a great alternative. Some supermarkets sell really big, fat, jumbo raisins and these are best for this recipe.

Serves 6

50 ml (2 fl oz) Muscat Beaumes de Venise, plus 1 tablespoon

1 tablespoon caster sugar

125 g (5 oz) muscatel raisins

450 g (1 lb) crowdie

For the oatmeal biscuits:

115 g (4½ oz) wholewheat flour

45 g (1½ oz) medium oatmeal

2 teaspoons soft light brown sugar

rounded ¼ teaspoon baking powder

a pinch of Maldon salt

75 g (3 oz) butter

1 tablespoon milk

Warm the 50 ml (2 fl oz) Muscat Beaumes de Venise and the sugar together in a small pan. Pour this over the raisins, cover and leave to soak overnight. Also, line six 7.5 cm (3 inch) metal pastry rings with small squares of damp muslin and set them on a fine-meshed cooling rack. Spoon in the cheese, level the surface and then cover with the overhanging muslin. Rest the rack over a baking tray, slide it into the fridge and leave the cheeses to drain overnight.

For the biscuits, preheat the oven to 180°C/350°F/Gas Mark 4. Mix the flour, oatmeal, sugar, baking powder and salt together in a bowl. Rub in the butter until the mixture looks like fine breadcrumbs. Stir in the milk to make a soft dough and knead very gently into a ball. On a work surface lightly dusted with flour, roll out the dough to a thickness of about 3 mm (¼ inch). Cut into 5 cm (2 inch) biscuits, rekneading and rolling the trimmings until you have about 24 biscuits. Place on a lightly greased baking sheet and prick a couple of times with a fork. Bake for 10–12 minutes until crisp and golden, then remove from the oven and leave to cool for 5 minutes. Transfer to a cooling rack and leave to go cold. Keep in an airtight tin if you make these the day before you need them.

Unmould the fresh cheeses into the centres of 6 small plates. Stir the 1 tablespoon of Muscat Beaumes de Venise into the raisins, then spoon some on top of and around the cheeses. Serve each cheese with about 4 of the oatmeal biscuits.

LIME AND PISTACHIO KULFI

with tropical fruits in a ginger and lemon grass syrup

Kulfi is an Indian ice-cream made from milk instead of cream. A large quantity of milk is slowly reduced in a large pan until you end up with real evaporated milk, which gives this finished dessert a lovely, rich flavour. I like to shape these puddings in dariole moulds, but rinsed yoghurt tubs work brilliantly too. The fruit salad adds a nice sharp contrast to the ice-creams.

Serves 6

2 litres (3 pints) full-cream milk
50 g (2 oz) shelled pistachio nuts
3 tablespoons caster sugar
½ teaspoon rosewater
15 g (½ oz) ground almonds
150 ml (5 fl oz) single cream
finely grated zest of 2 limes

For the tropical fruit salad:

120 ml (4 fl oz) cold water
50 g (2 oz) granulated sugar
½ stalk of lemon grass
pared zest of ½ lemon
pared zest of 1 lime
3 slices fresh root ginger
1 small sprig of fresh mint, plus very small leaves to decorate
225 g (8 oz) tropical fruits, such as mango, pawpaw, pineapple, kiwi fruit and bananas
2 tablespoons lime juice

Bring the milk to the boil in as large a pan as you have and leave it to simmer vigorously, stirring regularly to get rid of the skin as it forms and to make sure that it doesn't catch on the bottom of the pan. Do this for 1 hour or until it has reduced by two-thirds to about 700 ml (1¼ pints). Meanwhile, preheat the oven to 200°C/400°F/Gas Mark 6. Spread the pistachio nuts out on a tray and roast in the oven for 5 minutes until crisp. Leave to cool and then chop finely. Sprinkle some of the nuts in a thin layer on the base of 6 dariole moulds, small yoghurt pots or 7.5 cm (3 inch) ramekins.

Strain the reduced milk into a clean pan and stir in the sugar, rosewater and almonds. Simmer for 2–3 minutes more. Remove the pan from the heat and stir in the cream, the rest of the pistachio nuts and the lime zest. Leave the mixture to cool and then chill it in the fridge for 1 hour until really cold. Now churn the mixture in an ice-cream machine or pour it into a shallow plastic box and put it into the freezer, beating the mixture every now and then as it freezes to break up the ice crystals. When it is almost firm, spoon the mixture into the prepared moulds, cover with clingfilm and freeze until firm.

For the fruit salad, put the water and sugar into a small pan and leave over a low heat until the sugar has completely dissolved. Cut the lemon grass in half lengthways and bruise it lightly with the end of a rolling pin. Add half the lemon and lime zest, the lemon grass and ginger to the syrup and bring it up to the boil. Leave it to simmer for 5 minutes and then take it off the heat, add the sprig of mint and leave to cool. Strain the syrup into a bowl and chill in the fridge until really cold. Meanwhile, cut the rest of the lemon and lime zest into fine needle-shreds. Drop them into boiling water, leave for a few seconds and then drain and refresh under cold water. Set aside.

Just before serving, peel the fruits and cut them into small, neat pieces. Stir them into the chilled syrup with the lemon and lime shreds and the lime juice. Unmould the kulfi into the centres of 6 dessert plates and spoon around some of the tropical fruits and the syrup. Scatter the small mint leaves over the fruits and serve straight away.

DRAMBUIE ORANGES

This is one of my all-time favourite puddings and without a doubt one of the easiest – you can even make it in advance. Sometimes simple food is the best.

Serves 4

6–8 small, juicy, thin-skinned oranges
4 tablespoons Drambuie

Slice the top and the bottom off each orange and sit each one on a board. Cut away the outer skin so that there is no white pith left behind and then slice each orange across into thin slices. Arrange the slices overlapping in the centres of 4 large dessert plates, drizzle over the Drambuie and serve straight away. Alternatively, place the orange slices in a shallow dish with the Drambuie, cover and leave to chill in the fridge for 3–4 hours, during which time the juice from the oranges will develop a wonderful-tasting sauce with the Drambuie. Arrange on serving plates as before and serve while the slices are still chilled.

CRÈME FRAÎCHE TERRINE

with Calvados cream sauce and cidered pears

A big slice of vanilla-flavoured mousse with caramelized pears and a Calvados and caramel cream sauce – need I say more? All right – use ripe comice pears and don't eat too much in one sitting.

Serves 8-12

5 teaspoons powdered gelatine
450 ml (15 fl oz) natural yoghurt (whole-milk or Greek)
200 ml (7 fl oz) crème fraîche
75 g (3 oz) caster sugar
150 ml (5 fl oz) double cream
2 teaspoons vanilla extract
2 medium farm-fresh egg whites

For the Calvados cream sauce:

100 g (4 oz) caster sugar
300 ml (10 fl oz) double cream
3 tablespoons Calvados, Pommeau or brandy

For the cidered pears:

4–6 dessert pears
40 g (1½ oz) unsalted butter
3 tablespoons caster sugar
3 tablespoons dry cider

Put 5 tablespoons of cold water into a small pan. Sprinkle over the gelatine and leave it to 'sponge' for 5 minutes.

Mix the yoghurt, crème fraîche and sugar together in a large bowl until smooth. Lightly whip the cream until it begins to thicken and fold it into the yoghurt mixture with the vanilla extract. Place the pan of gelatine over a low heat and leave until clear. Stir it into the creamy mixture, making sure it is mixed in well. Whisk the egg whites in a separate bowl until they form soft peaks – the tips of the peaks should flop over, not stand upright. Fold 1 large spoonful into the yoghurt mixture to loosen it slightly, then gently fold in the remainder. Pour the mixture into a 7.5 cm (3 inch) deep, 7.5 × 25 cm (3 × 10 inch) terrine dish (a Le Creuset terrine is ideal), cover with clingfilm and chill in the fridge for at least 6 hours or preferably overnight.

For the Calvados cream sauce, put the sugar and 2 tablespoons of water into a pan and stir over a high heat until the sugar has dissolved. Now leave it to cook without stirring until it has turned a rich amber colour. Take the pan off the heat, pour in the cream and stir until all the caramel has dissolved into it – you might need to return it to a very low heat for a minute or two. Remove from the heat, leave to cool and then stir in the Calvados.

Just before you are ready to serve, cook the cidered pears. Cut the pears into quarters, remove the cores and then peel. Cut each piece in half once more. Melt the butter in a large, heavy-based frying pan and, as soon as it starts to foam, add the pears and fry over a high heat for 1 minute on each side until golden brown. Sprinkle over the sugar and the cider and continue to cook for no more than 2 minutes until the cider has reduced and formed a sugary syrup with the butter and sugar.

To serve, dip the terrine briefly into warm water. Invert it onto a serving plate or board and cut it into slices. Place one piece on each plate and arrange a few pieces of the cidered pears alongside. Pour the Calvados cream sauce over the terrine and the pears and serve immediately.

MUSCOVADO SUGAR MERINGUES

with lime cream and mangoes

It's important to use good-quality muscovado sugar here, and not that stuff which is just refined white sugar with a coating of molasses. I like Billington's sugars the best. Whatever you use, make sure you sieve it so that there are no lumps before you add it to the egg whites. When I was wee, meringues were a huge treat and I still insist on serving these up in the restaurant in big paper cases. It reminds me of a time when the thought of a meringue after tea would occupy my thoughts all day.

Serves 6

3 medium farm-fresh egg whites

175 g (6 oz) light muscovado sugar, sieved,
    plus a little extra for sprinkling

3 small ripe but firm mangoes

6 fresh mint sprigs, to decorate

For the lime cream:

300 ml (10 fl oz) double cream

finely grated zest of 2 limes

3 tablespoons lime juice (about 1½ limes)

1 tablespoon caster sugar

Preheat the oven to 110°C/225°F/Gas Mark ¼. Line a large baking sheet with non-stick baking parchment. Whisk the egg whites in a large, very clean bowl until they form stiff peaks. Very gradually whisk in the sugar, a spoonful at a time, making sure that you whisk the mixture well between each addition to ensure that the sugar has dissolved and combined with the egg whites. This is important in order to prevent the meringues from losing all their volume as muscovado sugar is quite moist and heavy.

Spoon the mixture into 6 meringues on the baking sheet and sprinkle the tops with a little more sugar. Bake for a minimum of 4 hours until very dry and hard. Cool and set aside.

To serve, peel the mangoes and then slice the flesh away from either side of the thin, flat stone in the centre. Cut each piece lengthways into long, thin slices. Whip the cream with the lime zest, lime juice and sugar until it forms soft peaks. Spoon a little of the cream into the centres of 6 dessert plates. Arrange slices of mango on top like the points of a star and then spoon on the rest of the cream. Place a meringue in the centre of each star and decorate with a sprig of mint.

HAZELNUT PAVLOVA CAKE

with raspberry cream

Ground nuts give a firmer texture and good, nutty flavour when added to the mix of a basic pavlova. Layered up with raspberries and whipped cream and dusted with icing sugar, it looks the part. It does need the fruit syrup to provide extra juice and zing, though. If you like, you could use pistachios instead of hazelnuts – these will give a lush green tinge to the finished meringue.

Serves 12

225 g (8 oz) shelled hazelnuts
300 g (10 oz) egg whites (from about
   8–10 farm-fresh medium eggs)
450 g (1lb) caster sugar
2 tablespoons balsamic vinegar
2 heaped teaspoons cornflour
450 ml (15 fl oz) double cream
3 tablespoons eau de framboises, eau de vie
   or Kirsch

3 tablespoons icing sugar, plus extra for dusting
350 g (12 oz) fresh raspberries

For the red fruit syrup:
120 ml (4 fl oz) Stock Syrup (see page 188)
225 g (8 oz) mixed summer fruits, such as
   strawberries, raspberries, blackberries,
   redcurrants and blackcurrants, prepared
   as necessary

Preheat the oven to 180°C/350°F/Gas Mark 4 and grease and base-line two 30 cm (12 inch) clip-sided cake tins with baking parchment. Spread the hazelnuts on a baking sheet and roast them in the oven for 10 minutes or so until they are richly golden. Leave to cool and then tip them into a clean tea towel and rub off the skins. Transfer the nuts to a food processor and give them a quick blitz for a few seconds until they are completely ground. Lower the oven temperature to 160°C/325°F/Gas Mark 3.

Place the egg whites in a large bowl or a food mixer and whisk them until they form soft peaks. Continue to whisk, adding the sugar a spoonful at a time. Make sure you mix the sugar thoroughly into the egg whites before you add the next spoonful. When all the sugar has been added, mix the balsamic vinegar with the cornflour and whisk this into the whites for 6–8 minutes until the meringue is very thick and shiny.

Fold the finely chopped hazelnuts into the meringue mixture, divide it evenly between the prepared tins and spread it out level with the back of a spoon. The mixture should be no more than 2 cm (¾ inch) thick. Bake the pavlovas in the preheated oven for 30 minutes until they have risen up and are lightly browned on top. Remove them from the oven and leave to cool for about 2 hours before removing them from their tins.

For the red fruit syrup, bring the stock syrup up to a simmer in a small pan. Add the summer fruits and cook gently for 15–20 minutes. Transfer the mixture to a liquidizer and blend until smooth. Pass the mixture through a fine sieve into a bowl and leave to cool. Then cover and chill until needed.

To assemble the pavlova, whip the cream with the eau de framboises, eau de vie or Kirsch and icing sugar into soft peaks. Gently fold in the raspberries so that they break up very slightly and the cream thickens a little more. Sandwich the two meringues together with the cream, transfer to a plate and leave in the fridge for 4 hours to firm up.

To serve, dust the top of the pavlova with icing sugar and cut it into 12 wedges. Lift them onto serving plates and serve with the red fruit syrup drizzled around the edges of the plates.

BUTTERSCOTCH TART

What could be more Scottish than butterscotch? The rich, smooth texture of the butterscotch-flavoured filling goes beautifully with my almost shortbread-like pastry so that all it needs is a just a little more cream to serve.

Serves 8

50 g (2 oz) butter
75 g (3 oz) soft light brown sugar
50 g (2 oz) granulated sugar
150 g (5 oz) golden syrup

300 ml (10 fl oz) double cream, plus extra for
   serving (optional)
1 teaspoon vanilla extract
4 medium farm-fresh eggs
1 × 25 cm (10 inch) Sweet Pastry tart case
   (see page 188)

Preheat the oven to 150°C/300°F/Gas Mark 2. For the filling, put the butter, soft brown sugar, granulated sugar and golden syrup into a medium-sized pan. Stir over a low heat until the sugars have dissolved and then cook gently for 5 minutes until smooth and thick. Remove the pan from the heat and stir in the double cream and the vanilla extract. Leave to cool for 10 minutes and then beat in the eggs. Strain the mixture into the pastry case and bake for 35–40 minutes until just set. Remove the tart from the oven and leave to cool for about 30 minutes. Cut it into wedges and serve with a little lightly whipped double cream if you wish.

DRAMBUIE CREAMS

with a raspberry and orange compote

Drambuie and oranges again – I can't get enough – but this time the Drambuie is used to flavour panna-cotta-like creams and served with a fresh-tasting combination of raspberries and orange juice.

Serves 6

300 ml (10 fl oz) double cream
225 ml (8 fl oz) milk
50 g (2 oz) caster sugar
2 teaspoons powdered gelatine or
   2½ x 3 g sheets leaf gelatine
4 tablespoons Drambuie liqueur

For the raspberry and orange compote:
450 g (1 lb) fresh raspberries
50 g (2 oz) caster sugar
finely grated zest of ½ orange
50 ml (2 fl oz) freshly squeezed orange juice

For the Drambuie creams, soak the leaf gelatine, if using, in cold water for a few minutes. Put the cream, milk, sugar and leaf gelatine into a pan and leave over a low heat until the sugar and gelatine have dissolved. If using powdered gelatine, put 2 tablespoons of cold water into a small pan. Sprinkle over the gelatine and leave to 'sponge' for 5 minutes. Place the pan over a low heat and leave until the gelatine is clear. Stir into the cream and milk mixture, followed by the Drambuie. Pour the mixture into 6 dariole moulds or 7.5 cm (3 inch) ramekins, cover and chill for 4 hours or until set.

For the raspberry and orange compote, put 225 g (8 oz) of the raspberries into a bowl with the sugar and the orange zest and crush with the back of a fork into a smooth purée. Press the mixture through a fine sieve into a bowl to remove all the seeds, stir in the orange juice and chill in the fridge for 1 hour or until needed.

To serve, dip the dariole moulds or ramekins very briefly into warm water. Unmould the creams into the centre or slightly to one side of each dessert plate. Stir the rest of the raspberries into the raspberry and orange sauce and spoon some around the creams.

FREE-FORMED APPLE TARTS

with mincemeat ice-cream

Free-form apple tarts have an organic, rustic appearance which appeals to me and it means you don't need any special tins. These tarts are dead easy to make.

Serves 6

1 quantity Sweet Pastry (see page 188)
900 g (2 lb) firm dessert apples, such as Cox's
   or Egremont Russets
50 g (2 oz) soft light brown sugar
1 teaspoon ground cinnamon
¼ teaspoon each freshly grated nutmeg and
   ground cloves
1 medium farm-fresh egg white
2 tablespoons semolina
2 tablespoons caster sugar

For the mincemeat ice-cream:

175 g (6 oz) mixed dried fruits or a mixture of
   sultanas, currants, raisins and chopped
   candied peel
5 tablespoons dark rum
600 ml (1 pint) milk
6 medium farm-fresh egg yolks
50 g (2 oz) caster sugar
250 ml (8 fl oz) double cream
40 g (1½ oz) toasted chopped almonds

For the ice-cream, put the mixed dried fruits and rum together into a bowl. Cover and set to one side for a few hours to allow the fruits to soak up all the rum. Bring the milk to the boil in a pan. Whisk the egg yolks and sugar together in a bowl until pale and creamy. Pour on the hot milk, whisk together well and return the mixture to the pan. Cook over a gentle heat, stirring, until it lightly coats the back of a wooden spoon. Stir in the double cream and leave to cool, then chill in the fridge for about 1 hour until really cold. Now you can either churn the mixture in an ice-cream machine, adding the rum-soaked fruits and toasted, chopped almonds a few minutes before the end, or pour it into a shallow plastic box and leave in the freezer until almost firm. If doing the latter, scrape the mixture into a food processor and whizz it until smooth – this will break down all the ice crystals in the mixture. Scrape the mixture back into the box, return it to the freezer and leave once more until almost firm. Repeat the whizzing process once more, stir in the rum-soaked fruits and toasted, chopped almonds and leave in the freezer until really firm or until required.

For the apple tarts, preheat the oven to 200°C/400°F/Gas Mark 6. Quarter the apples, and core and then peel them. Slice thickly into a bowl and stir in the sugar and the spices. Divide the pastry into 6 equal pieces and, on a lightly floured board, roll each one out into a 18 cm (7 inch) disc. Brush each disc with a little of the unbeaten egg white and then sprinkle 1 teaspoon of the semolina into the centre of each one, leaving a 5 cm (2 inch) border around the edge free. Pile the apple mixture into the centre and then fold the edges of the pastry over the fruit, leaving some of the fruit showing in the middle and pleating the pastry as you go to keep it in place.

Carefully lift the tarts onto a lightly buttered baking sheet and chill for 30 minutes. Brush the edges of the tarts with more of the unbeaten egg white and then sprinkle with the caster sugar. Bake the tarts for 25–30 minutes until the pastry is golden and the apples are cooked. Slide onto dessert plates and serve with scoops of the mincemeat ice-cream.

MACERATED STRAWBERRIES

with basil and white pepper ice-cream

An intriguing combination this, but strawberries, basil and pepper really do work together. Talking about pepper, why is it so difficult to buy white peppercorns? The only place that I ever seem to have success is the local Indian grocer's shop. Supermarkets everywhere, please take heed and stock them now!

Serves 6-8

750–900 g (1½–2 lb) strawberries

2 tablespoons caster sugar

1 tablespoon eau de fraise, eau de vie
  or Kirsch

12 fresh basil leaves, very finely shredded

For the white pepper ice-cream:

1 teaspoon white peppercorns

600 ml (1 pint) milk

6 medium farm-fresh egg yolks

75 g (3 oz) caster sugar

250 ml (8 fl oz) double cream

For the ice-cream, crush the peppercorns with a pestle and mortar or in a mug using the end of a rolling pin. Tip them into a tea strainer or small fine sieve and sift away all the fine powder so that you are left with just very small crumbs of pepper. Bring the milk to the boil in a pan. Whisk the egg yolks and sugar together in a bowl until pale and creamy. Pour on the hot milk, whisk together well and return the mixture to the pan. Cook over a gentle heat, stirring, until it lightly coats the back of a wooden spoon. Pour into a bowl and leave to cool. Then stir in the double cream and pepper and chill in the fridge for about 1 hour until the mixture is really cold. Now you can either churn the mixture in an ice-cream machine or pour it into a shallow plastic box and leave it in the freezer until almost firm. If doing the latter, scrape the mixture into a food processor and whizz it until smooth – this will break down all the ice crystals in the mixture. Scrape the mixture back into the box, return to the freezer and leave once more until almost firm. Repeat the whizzing process once more and then leave in the freezer until really firm or until required.

Hull the strawberries and slice them in half into a bowl. Stir in the sugar, eau de fraise, eau de vie or Kirsch and basil, cover and chill in the fridge for 15–30 minutes. Serve the strawberries in dessert bowls with scoops of the white pepper ice-cream.

MY MUM'S PANCAKES

with a choice of preserves

A lovely dessert or perfect for afternoon tea. A little clotted cream wouldn't go amiss either. The preserves make far more than you need for one sitting but also taste great on toast or ordinary warm scones.

Serves 4

For the pancakes:

75 g (3 oz) self-raising flour

1 teaspoon baking powder

50 g (2 oz) granulated sugar

1 farm-fresh egg

150 ml (5 fl oz) milk

a little butter, to serve

For the whisky and rhubarb preserve:

1.5 kg (3 lb) wild or cultivated rhubarb

900 g (2 lb) sugar

finely grated zest of 1 lemon

175 ml (6 fl oz) best Islay whisky

For Aunty Ulla's no-cook marmalade:

225 g (8 oz) dried apricots, washed

1 lemon

2 oranges

450 g (1 lb) caster sugar

First make the preserves. For the whisky and rhubarb preserve, cut off either end of each piece of rhubarb and wipe the stalks clean with a cloth – there's no need to peel them. Cut them into 2.5 cm (1 inch) long chunks. Layer the rhubarb and sugar in a large, deep bowl or dish and leave to stand for 24 hours, by which time the sugar should have changed into a liquid state. Pour the sugary liquid into a preserving pan and add the grated lemon zest. Bring to the boil and boil briskly for 30 minutes. Now add the rhubarb and boil for another 30 minutes. Take the pan off the heat and stir in the whisky. Place the pan near a hot oven or an open fire and leave it to stand for a further 30 minutes. Then spoon the preserve into sterilized jars, cover with waxed discs and seal.

For Aunty Ulla's no-cook marmalade, you will need to soak the dried apricots overnight. The next day, drain them and mince them in a mincer or give them a whizz in a food processor. Scrub the lemon and the oranges, then drop them into a pan of boiling water and scald for 1 minute. Remove and, when cooled slightly, cut them in half and squeeze out the juice. Mince or whizz the flesh and mix this with the juice, the sugar and the minced apricots. Pack the mixture in a large sterilized jar. You can use it straight away but it's best kept for 2–3 days to allow the flavour to mature.

For the pancakes, sift the flour and baking powder into a bowl and stir in the granulated sugar. Whisk the egg and then stir it into the dry ingredients – it is very important that you don't beat it in. Then whisk in enough milk to give a batter which has the consistency of double cream.

Heat a smooth, cast-iron griddle over a medium–high heat. Test the heat by sprinkling the griddle with a little flour. If it browns straight away, it is too hot. If it takes a few seconds before it browns, then it's perfect.

Drop 3 tablespoonfuls of the batter, spaced a little apart, onto the griddle. When bubbles appear on the tops of the pancakes and they are golden brown underneath – about 2–3 minutes – turn them over using a palette knife, and cook for another 2 minutes until golden brown on the other side. Lift them off onto a plate, cover with a cloth and keep warm while you cook the rest. You should make about 12 pancakes. Then simply serve them spread with a little butter and some preserve.

FRUIT SCONE AND BUTTER PUDDINGS

The idea for this came from my noticing that an average scone fits perfectly inside a 7.5 cm (3 inch) ramekin. Don't ask how that particular thought occurred to me – many and mysterious are the ways of a chef's brain! However, scones do make excellent individual puddings which can be made up in advance and reheated if you wish. The rest of the scones are fantastic split and served with strawberry jam and clotted cream, or just butter.

Serves 6

50 g (2 oz) sultanas

50 g (2 oz) dried apricots, chopped into
   small pieces

50 ml (2 fl oz) good whisky

1 vanilla pod

300 ml (10 fl oz) milk

300 ml (10 fl oz) double cream

5 medium farm-fresh egg yolks

50 g (2 oz) caster sugar

75 g (3 oz) butter for spreading

4 tablespoons warm sieved apricot jam

For the fruit scones:

225 g (8 oz) self-raising flour

½ teaspoon salt

1 teaspoon baking powder

40 g (1½ oz) unsalted butter

50 g (2 oz) raisins, or currants, sultanas,
   chopped dates, etc.

40 g (1½ oz) caster sugar

150 ml (5 fl oz) milk

beaten egg or milk, to glaze

Place the sultanas, apricots and whisky in a small bowl, cover and leave to soak, overnight if possible or for a minimum of 2 hours.

The next day, make the scones. Slide a baking sheet into the oven and preheat it to 230°C/450°F/Gas Mark 8. Sift the flour, salt and baking powder into a bowl and then rub in the butter until the mixture looks like fine breadcrumbs. Stir in the dried fruits and the sugar. Make a well in the centre and stir in enough milk to give a soft dough – make sure the mixture is not too dry or the scones will end up like little rocks! Turn the mixture out onto a lightly floured surface and knead briefly to remove any cracks from the mixture. Then gently roll it out (or pat it out with your hands if you prefer) until the dough is about 2 cm (¾ inch) thick. Cut out 10–12 rounds using a 5 cm (2 inch) cutter dipped in flour. Brush with egg or milk, place on the hot baking sheet and bake towards the top of the oven for 8–10 minutes until the scones are well risen and brown. Transfer to a wire rack and leave to cool. Reduce the oven temperature to 180°C/350°F/Gas Mark 4.

Cut the vanilla pod in half and scrape out the seeds into a pan. Add the milk and the cream and bring to the boil very slowly. Remove the vanilla pod.

Cream the egg yolks and sugar together in a bowl and then whisk in two-thirds of the hot milk and cream. Mix together well, return to the pan containing the remaining milk and cream mix. Cook over a gentle heat, stirring all the time, until the mixture lightly coats the back of a wooden spoon. Pour into a jug and set aside.

Very thinly slice the baked top and bottom off 6 of the scones and discard. These are the scones you will be using for the puddings. (Store the remaining scones in an airtight container; they will keep for 3 days.) Cut each of the 6 scones into 3 slices and spread each slice quite heavily with butter.

Place one scone slice in the bottom of a greased 7.5 cm (3 inch) ramekin and sprinkle over a few of the soaked sultanas and apricots. Pour over a little of the custard mix to cover. Repeat twice more so that the ramekin is filled to the top. Repeat the process with 5 more ramekins. Set aside for ¾–1 hour.

Sit the ramekins in a roasting tin and pour in hot water until it comes half-way up the sides of the dishes. Bake for 40 minutes until set and lightly golden. Remove the ramekins from the roasting tin, brush the puddings with a little of the warmed apricot jam and serve straight away.

HOT TODDIE SOUFFLÉS

While mucking about with the idea of using hot toddie flavourings in various puddings, I struck on the idea of the hot toddie soufflé. Out of the range of ideas I tried – mousse, tart, ice-cream, etc. – this was by far the best. So here's the recipe for your delectation. As with all soufflés, butter the mould well and don't overwhisk the egg whites.

Serves 6

a little butter for greasing
40 g (1½ oz) caster sugar, plus extra for
    dusting
50 ml (2 fl oz) whisky
1 teaspoon finely grated lemon zest
1 tablespoon lemon juice

3 whole cloves
300 ml (10 fl oz) milk
3 medium farm-fresh egg yolks
15 g (½ oz) plain flour
15 g (½ oz) cornflour
4 tablespoons clear honey
6 medium farm-fresh egg whites
icing sugar, to decorate

Slide a baking sheet onto the middle shelf of the oven and preheat it to 220°C/425°F/ Gas Mark 7. Grease six 7.5 cm (3 inch) ramekins with butter, making sure that you take it right up to the top of the rim, and dust them out with some of the caster sugar.

Put the whisky, lemon zest, lemon juice and cloves into a small pan and leave over a low heat. Pour the milk into another pan and bring it up to the boil. Mix the egg yolks, the 40 g (1½ oz) caster sugar, flour and cornflour together in a bowl until smooth. Whisk in the boiling milk, return the mixture to the pan and cook over a gentle heat, stirring every now and then, for 10 minutes so that you cook out the taste of the flour. Strain the whisky mixture into the custard, add 1 tablespoon of the honey and whisk together well.

Whisk the egg whites in a large clean bowl into soft peaks. Gradually whisk in the rest of the honey to make a soft meringue. Lightly whisk one-quarter of the honey meringue into the custard to loosen it slightly, then carefully fold in the remainder. Spoon the mixture into the prepared ramekins, level the tops and then run the tip of a knife around the inside edge of each dish to release the mixture. Slide the ramekins onto the baking sheet and bake for 10–12 minutes until the soufflés are well risen, browned and doubled in height but still slightly wobbly. Quickly lift them onto small dessert plates, dust with icing sugar and serve straight away.

BASICS

MARINATED VEGETABLE STOCK

This stock freezes well and the ingredients are always reasonably easy to get. Freeze it in small tubs so that you can defrost the required quantity as and when you need it.

Makes about
1.2 litres (2 pints)

1 large onion
1 leek, cleaned
2 sticks celery
1 fennel bulb (optional)
4 large carrots

1 head garlic, cut across its equator
8 white peppercorns
1 teaspoon pink peppercorns (optional)
1 teaspoon coriander seeds
1 piece star anise
1 fresh bay leaf
40 g (1½ oz) mixed fresh herbs
300 ml (10 fl oz) dry white wine

Chop all the vegetables into 1 cm (½ inch) dice, place in a large pan and cover with water. Add the garlic, peppercorns, coriander seeds, star anise and bay leaf, bring to the boil and simmer for 8 minutes. Add the fresh herbs and simmer for a further 3 minutes. Now add the white wine and remove from the heat. Cover and leave to marinate somewhere cool for 48 hours. Then strain through a fine sieve and use immediately, or freeze and use within 6 weeks.

FISH STOCK

Good fish stock should form a slight jelly consistency. In the summer, it's best to freeze stock immediately but in the winter it will keep for 48 hours in the fridge.

Makes about 300 ml (10 fl oz)

750 g (1½ lb) fish bones, preferably sole,
   turbot or brill
1.2 litres (2 pints) cold water
½ medium-sized onion, finely diced
1 white of leek, finely diced
1 celery stick, finely diced
6 white peppercorns
½ fresh bay leaf
15 g (½oz) fresh herbs, such as chervil,
   parsley, tarragon and coriander
1 tablespoon olive oil
300 ml (10 fl oz) dry white wine

Soak the fish bones in cold water for half an hour. Drain, wash and roughly chop.

In a medium-sized saucepan, gently sweat all of the finely diced vegetables, peppercorns, bay leaf and herbs in the olive oil until soft, but without colouring them. Add the white wine and boil until nearly dry. Now add the fish bones and stir to coat. Pour over enough cold water just to cover the mixture (about 1.2 litres/2 pints). Bring it to the boil, skim and then simmer for about 18 minutes (do not allow to boil). Remove it from the heat and allow to stand until cool (this takes about 3-4 hours).

Once cooled, pour the stock through a sieve or colander, then pass it through a fine sieve into a tall container. Place in the fridge and leave it overnight to allow it to settle.

The next day, skim off any scum that has settled on the top, then spoon off all the clear jellied stock, which should then be frozen until needed.

You may notice some white gunge at the bottom of the container. This should not be considered edible and should be discarded.

CHICKEN STOCK

There is nothing to compare with a good home-made chicken stock and it is invaluable in the kitchen. Use uncooked chicken carcasses, not ones left over from the Sunday roast, to ensure you get that lovely fresh flavour.

Makes 1.25 litres (2¼ pints)

3 chicken carcasses, skin and fat removed
1 large carrot, quartered
2 medium leeks, cleaned
2 sticks celery, halved lengthways
1 unpeeled onion, quartered
1 small head garlic, cut across its equator
6 white peppercorns
1 fresh bay leaf
1 sprig of fresh thyme
15 g (½ oz) fresh parsley or tarragon stalks

Place the carcasses in a large pan that they only half fill. Just cover with about 2.25 litres (4 pints) of cold water and bring to the boil, skimming off any scum as it rises to the surface. Skim off any fat, then place the rest of the ingredients in a thick layer over the top of the carcasses. Adjust the heat to a simmer and leave to cook for 3–4 hours, during which time the vegetables will act like a filter, absorbing all the gunk and leaving you with a crystal clear stock. Taste the stock every now and then while it's cooking. When you notice that the flavour stops improving, your stock is ready.

Strain the stock into another pan through a colander, and then once more through a chinois or fine sieve into a tall container or large jug. Cover and leave to cool, then chill in the fridge overnight. The next day, skim any fat off the surface and use as required, or freeze to use later.

BEEF STOCK

Making a good beef stock is a time-consuming business as it has to be simmered for 8 hours, but it's a must for jus sauces – namely those made only of well-reduced stocks. It gives them plenty of body and prevents them from being too watery.

Makes 1.2 litres (2 pints)

4.5 kg (10 lb) beef knuckle bones
2 large carrots, cut into 2.5 cm (1 inch) pieces
2 large unpeeled onions, cut into 8 wedges
2 large leeks, cleaned and cut into 2.5 cm (1 inch) pieces
2 sticks celery, cut into 2.5 cm (1 inch) pieces
1 head garlic, cut across its equator
15 g (½ oz) fresh parsley or tarragon stalks
1 fresh bay leaf
1 large sprig of fresh thyme
12 black peppercorns
3 plum tomatoes, quartered
2 tablespoons tomato purée
300 ml (10 fl oz) red wine
1 pig's trotter
450 g (1 lb) shin of beef

Preheat the oven to 200°C/400°F/Gas Mark 6. Place the beef bones in a large roasting tray, slide them into the hot oven and roast for about 1 hour until well browned. Tip off the marrow fat and reserve.

Heat a large stock pot until very hot and add 3 tablespoons of the marrow fat (which should smoke as soon as it hits the hot pan). Add all the vegetables (except the tomatoes), the garlic, herbs and peppercorns and stir over a high heat until well browned – it is important to achieve a good, dark colour, but without burning.

Add the tomatoes and the tomato purée and cook until the tomatoes have reduced to a thick pulp. Add the wine and boil until it has almost all disappeared. Now add the roasted beef bones, the pig's trotter and the shin of beef and cover with cold water. Bring to the boil, skimming the scum off the surface as it appears, then reduce the heat so that the liquid barely trembles and leave to simmer for 8 hours, or preferably overnight.

Strain the stock into another pan and leave to cool. Once cold, skim off any fat, strain once more through a chinois or fine sieve into another pan and bring back to the boil. Continue to boil until reduced by half and then leave to cool. Use or freeze as required.

BALSAMIC VINEGAR SYRUP

This process intensifies the flavour of the vinegar and also makes it thick and syrupy so that it looks great when drizzled over a plate, especially with a little oil. It is excellent drizzled over roasted vegetables, a Parma ham salad, rocket leaves, or anything vaguely Italian. When you're making it, ensure the kitchen is well ventilated as the vinegary fumes can make your eyes water. And use middle-of-the-road vinegar for this recipe, not your best 10-year-old vinegar.

1 bottle balsamic vinegar

Bring the vinegar to the boil in a pan and leave it to simmer quite vigorously until it has reduced by about half and become thick and syrupy. Watch it towards the end as you don't want it to go too far and burn. Leave to cool, then store in an airtight bottle. It will keep indefinitely.

CLARIFIED BUTTER

Clarified butter is the oily part of the butter, that is, without the buttermilk and is excellent for frying potatoes to give them a rich buttery colour. You can buy it ready prepared in Indian delicatessens (as *ghee*).

Makes about 200 ml (7 fl oz)   *250 g (9 oz) butter*

In a small pan, melt the butter on a low heat. Allow it to stand for a few minutes until all the oil rises to the top, then skim off the scum that has risen to the surface. Pour off the clear oil into a small bowl, leaving behind the milky-white solids which will have collected at the bottom. Discard the milky-white solids. The oil will keep in the fridge for 2–3 days.

TOMATOES CONCASSÉES

Skinned, deseeded and neatly diced tomatoes that have had all their acidic juices removed can be used for all sorts of salads and sauces. Their success will depend on the quality of the plum tomatoes you use.

firm, ripe, plum tomatoes

Remove the skins of the tomatoes. You can do this in one of two ways:

Hot water: Cut a little, shallow cross in the top of each tomato, place them in a bowl and cover with boiling water. Leave for about 30 seconds, drain and cover with cold water. The skins should come off quite easily.

Naked flame: Spear the tomatoes onto a fork or skewer, place them near a naked flame – the gas burner of your stove or a blowtorch – and turn them until the skins start to blacken and blister. Then peel.

Cut the peeled tomatoes into quarters, scoop out the seeds and cut the flesh into very neat 5 mm (¼ inch) dice. They are best used immediately but will keep refrigerated for up to 24 hours.

HOME-DRIED TOMATOES

Makes 24 pieces

12 large, ripe plum tomatoes
Maldon salt and freshly ground white pepper

50 ml (2 fl oz) olive oil plus extra for preserving
1 sprig of fresh basil or thyme
1 clove garlic, crushed

Preheat the oven to 110°C/225°F/Gas Mark ¼. Slice the tomatoes in half lengthways and remove the little green 'eyes' from the stalk ends. Place the tomatoes cut-side up on a baking sheet and sprinkle with crushed salt and 12 turns of the pepper mill. Drizzle over the 50 ml (2 fl oz) olive oil.

Place the tomatoes in the oven and leave for 8 hours, by which time they should have shrunk to half their original size but not browned. Turn them over and leave for a further 4 hours or until they are nice and firm.

Remove them from the oven and leave to go cold. Then pack them with the basil or thyme and garlic into a sterilized jar that holds about 600 ml (1 pint) and cover in olive oil. Seal and store in the fridge for up to 3 weeks.

ROASTED RED PEPPERS

Use large, ripe red peppers here. The secret of success is to get the skin of the pepper really blackened without burning the flesh underneath.

6 large red peppers
olive oil
1 clove garlic

1 sprig of fresh thyme
1 fresh bay leaf

There are three ways of skinning peppers:

Oven roasting: Preheat the oven to 240°C/475°F/Gas Mark 9. Place the peppers directly on the oven rack and put a baking tray on the rack underneath to collect any dripping juices. Roast the peppers, turning them once or twice, for 10–15 minutes, or until their skins are blistered and blackened.

Grilling: Preheat your grill to its highest setting. Rub a little olive oil over the outside of the peppers, place them on the rack of the grill pan and grill them, turning them as they colour, until they are blackened all over.

Naked flame: Spear the peppers onto a fork or skewer, place them near a naked flame – the gas burner of your stove or a blowtorch – and turn them until they are blackened all over.

Drop the peppers into a plastic bag and seal, or wrap tightly in clingfilm, and leave to cool. Unwrap the peppers, cut them open and scoop out the seeds. Then carefully peel off the skins, which will come away quite easily, and use the flesh as required.

If you don't want to use the peppers straight away, pack them into a sterilized jar with the garlic, thyme and bay leaf. Cover with olive oil, seal and store in the fridge for up to 2 weeks.

HERB OIL

If you prize colour and fragrance in your meals, this is for you. You could also make it with individual herbs instead of a mixture. Chive oil retains its grassy colour better than any other, while the aroma of basil oil is unmistakable and guaranteed to lift your mood. Herb oil has a fabulous colour and makes a great garnish to many dishes.

Makes about 300 ml (10 fl oz)

40 g (1½ oz) mixed fresh herbs, such as
chives, parsley, chervil, tarragon and dill
300 ml (10 fl oz) olive oil

Drop the herbs into a pan of heavily salted boiling water and leave for just 10 seconds to set the colour. Drain and refresh under cold water to stop the cooking process, then drain and wring out well in a clean tea towel. Chop up roughly and place in a liquidizer with the oil. Blitz for 2–3 minutes. Pour into a sterilized bottle, seal and refrigerate. Shake before using and keep for up to 1 week.

CHILLI OIL

This stuff is mega spicy but, used sparingly, it imparts a wonderful glow to many dishes and looks stunning drizzled around the edge of a plate as garnish.

Makes about 300 ml (10 fl oz)

50 g (2 oz) ripe, red chillies, preferably
Scotch bonnets
1 large red pepper, seeded
300 ml (10 fl oz) sunflower oil

Slice the chillies in half lengthways and roughly chop the red pepper. Place in a pan with the oil, carefully bring to the boil and leave to simmer gently for 10 minutes. Remove from the heat and leave to cool.

Once cold, transfer to a sealable plastic or glass container and leave in a cool place for 2–3 weeks. Then pour the oil through a fine sieve into a bottle and use as required.

CURRY OIL

This oil has a wonderful amber colour and aromatic taste which can be used for cooking dishes of a similar nature, as well as for garnishing numerous spicy dishes.

Makes about 300 ml (10 fl oz)

300 ml (10 fl oz) olive oil
1 teaspoon coriander seeds
1 teaspoon cumin seeds

1 cm (½ inch) piece fresh root ginger, bruised and then very finely chopped
1 clove garlic
1 tablespoon good-quality curry paste

Heat 2 tablespoons of the oil in a pan. Add the spices, ginger and garlic and cook over a medium heat for about 1 minute. Add the curry paste and cook for another 30 seconds. Add the rest of the oil and simmer for 5 minutes. Leave to cool and then transfer to a bottle, seal and store in a cool, dark place until needed. Shake before using.

LOBSTER OR SHELLFISH OIL

This is quite extravagant but does add a wonderful flavour to many fish and seafood dishes. It's also a great way of making use of all those shells that are usually just discarded.

Makes about 300 ml (10 fl oz)

175 g (6 oz) lobster or langoustine shells
350 ml (12 fl oz) sunflower oil
1 tiny piece broken star anise
3 white peppercorns
5 cm (2 inch) piece carrot, peeled and diced

2 shallots, diced
5 cm (2 inch) piece celery, diced
2 cloves garlic
15 g (½ oz) mixed fresh herbs such as, parsley, thyme and tarragon
½ teaspoon tomato purée
50 ml (2 fl oz) dry white wine

Crush the shells and drain away any liquid. Heat 4 tablespoons of the oil in a pan, add the shells, star anise and white peppercorns and fry over a medium heat for about 15 minutes, stirring every now and then. Add all the remaining ingredients, except the oil, and cook until the wine has evaporated. Add the rest of the oil and leave to simmer for 45 minutes. Remove from the heat and leave to stand for 24 hours. Strain through a muslin-lined sieve, transfer to a bottle and seal. This will keep in the fridge for about 1 month.

SWEET PASTRY

Makes about 450 g (1 lb),
enough to line one 25 cm (10 inch) tart tin
or 6 x 10 cm (4 inch) tartlet tins

*175 g (6 oz) unsalted butter, at room
temperature*

50 g (2 oz) caster sugar
a pinch of Maldon salt
250 g (9 oz) plain flour
1 medium farm-fresh egg yolk
1 tablespoon cold water

Cream the butter, sugar and salt together in a bowl until light and fluffy (you can do this with an electric mixer or in a food processor). Add 50 g (2 oz) of the flour and mix in. Now add the egg yolk and slowly mix in the rest of the flour a spoonful at a time until it is all incorporated. Add the water and mix for another 15 seconds.

Turn the dough onto a lightly floured surface and knead briefly (3 or 4 times) until smooth. Wrap in clingfilm and chill in the fridge for at least 3 hours before using.

Slide a baking sheet into the oven and preheat it to 200°C/400°F/Gas Mark 6. Remove the pastry from the fridge and knead briefly once more until smooth.

For one 25 cm (10 inch) pastry case: Roll out the pastry to a thickness of about 3mm (¼ inch) on a floured surface and use to line a lightly greased tart tin. Leave the excess pastry overhanging and line with greaseproof paper and baking beans. Chill in the fridge for 15 minutes. Now slide the case onto the baking sheet and bake for 11 minutes. Remove the paper and beans and bake the case for a further 9 minutes or until the pastry is lightly browned. Neatly slice away the overhanging pastry and leave the case to cool and then use when required.

For six tartlet cases: Cut the pastry into 6 even pieces, roll out and use to line 6 lightly greased 10 cm (4 inch) tartlet tins. Line with greaseproof paper and beans, chill for 15 minutes and then bake as before.

STOCK SYRUP

Makes 1.25 litres (2¼ pints)

1 kg (2¼ lb) granulated sugar
1 litre (1¾ pints) water

Put the sugar and water into a medium-sized pan and place over a high heat. Bring to the boil, stirring from time to time. Leave the syrup to simmer for 5 minutes before skimming off any impurities that may have risen to the surface. Leave to cool and use as required.

INDEX

Page references to illustrations are in *italic*